CHILD DEVELOPMENT DURING THE ELEMENTARY SCHOOL YEARS

ABOUT THE AUTHORS

Although father-daughter writing teams are not unknown, they are rather rare. Joy N. Humphrey, an elementary school classroom teacher, received her graduate degree from The Johns Hopkins University. This is the seventh book she has co-authored with her father. In addition, she has published several invited chapters in various books. She serves on the board of reviewers for *Advancements in Health Education,* an annual research publication.

James H. Humphrey, Professor Emeritus at the University of Maryland, has been a recognized authority on child development and learning for over three decades. He has published over 40 books and 200 articles and research reports.

CHILD DEVELOPMENT DURING THE ELEMENTARY SCHOOL YEARS

By

JOY N. HUMPHREY, M.S.

Garden City Public Schools
Garden City , Michigan

and

JAMES H. HUMPHREY, ED.D.

Professor Emeritus
University of Maryland

With a Foreword by

Michael Wilmot, ED.D.

Superintendent of Schools
Garden City, Michigan

CHARLES C THOMAS • PUBLISHER
Springfield • Illinois • U.S.A.

Published and Distributed Throughout the World by

CHARLES C THOMAS • PUBLISHER
2600 South First Street
Springfield, Illinois 62794-9265

© *1989 by* CHARLES C THOMAS • PUBLISHER

ISBN 0-398-05622-6

Library of Congress Catalog Card Number: 89-36312

With THOMAS BOOKS *careful attention is given to all details of manufacturing
and design. It is the Publisher's desire to present books that are satisfactory as to their
physical qualities and artistic possibilities and appropriate for their particular use.*
THOMAS BOOKS *will be true to those laws of quality that assure a good name
and good will.*

Printed in the United States of America
SC-R-3

Library of Congress Cataloging-in-Publication Data
Humphrey, Joy N.
    Child development during the elementary school years / by Joy N.
Humphrey and James H. Humphrey ; with a foreword by Michael Wilmot.
        p.   cm.
    Includes bibliographical references.
    ISBN 0-398-05622-6
    1. Child development.   I. Humphrey, James Harry, 1911-
II. Title.
LB1115.H83   1989
305.23'1 — dc20   89-36312
                                                                       CIP

FOREWORD

The challenge facing today's elementary schools is greater than at any prior time. The information explosion, the rapid development of technology, dramatic changes in the structure of the American family, increased demands for higher levels of student achievement, a variety of social issues, and the expectation that the schools teach everything from basic skills to personal values all contribute to make the use of a *total development* approach to elementary education a necessity.

Research related to instructional techniques has clearly shown that the selection of learning objectives at the appropriate developmental level for the student is basic to designing effective learning experiences. Therefore, a thorough understanding of the process by which children develop is a requisite for those who have the responsibility of instructing elementary school children.

Child Development During the Elementary School Years by Joy N. Humphrey and James H. Humphrey provides an in-depth analysis of the *total development* process. The book examines the physical, motor, social, emotional, and intellectual development of elementary school-age children. Guidelines for development, factors involved with development, and various implications of development on the educational process are presented. Factors which influence the development of children, such as stress and general health, are also discussed. The inclusion of numerous suggestions for developmentally appropriate learning experiences are provided along with specific examples to assist teachers, parents, and others concerned with the development of children.

The task of assisting elementary school children, as they develop into responsible citizens who can think critically and independently, is a difficult one. This task is made easier, however, by the Humphreys' most recent book. Classroom teachers, parents, and all others interested in helping children learn and develop will find this book a tremendous resource.

MICHAEL WILMOT

v

PREFACE

Child Development During the Elementary School Years should serve at least two major purposes: first, it should be a suitable text for college and university courses in child development; second, it should find use as an important source book for teachers, parents, and other adults who deal in some way with children of elementary school age.

The initial chapter gives an overview of child development, taking into account the meaning of terms as well as presenting a concept of *total* development.

Chapter 2, in discussing physical development, departs from a traditional approach concerned only with anatomical and physiological aspects. On the other hand, physical needs of children are discussed along with ways of meeting these needs.

The third chapter is about motor development and takes into account locomotor skills, axial skills, and skills of retrieval and propulsion. There are explanations of how to perform these skills and the conditions under which they are used.

In chapter 4, social development is approached from the standpoint of social needs of children along with ways of meeting these needs. Also discussed are ways to evaluate social interactions of children.

Chapter 5 is concerned with emotions and how they influence the development of the child. Considered are both pleasant and unpleasant emotions. Also a rating scale is presented for use in evaluating the extent to which the school environment contributes to emotional development of the child.

In chapter 6, guidelines for intellectual development of the different types of learners are discussed. Included here are the different classifications of slow learners as well as gifted and talented children.

Children in modern society are under a great deal of stress in both the home and school. Many of these concerns are addressed in Chapter 7 and a concept of stress is presented.

One of the most important factors in the development of children is

vii

that they maintain a suitable level of health. In the final chapter such areas as nutrition and diet, sleep and rest, and physical activity and exercise are discussed in terms of how they impact on child development during the elementary school years. The various aspects of school health are also taken into account.

JOY N. HUMPHREY
JAMES H. HUMPHREY

CONTENTS

CHILD DEVELOPMENT DURING THE ELEMENTARY SCHOOL YEARS

Chapter 1

AN OVERVIEW OF CHILD DEVELOPMENT

A long-standing definition states that *child development is an interdisciplinary approach to the study of children, drawing upon such sciences as biology, physiology, embryology, pediatrics, sociology, psychiatry, anthropology, and psychology; emphasis is placed on the importance of understanding children through study of their mental, emotional, social, and physical growth; particular emphasis is laid on the appraisal of the impacts on the growing personality of home, school, and community.*[1] Although this definition applies to children of all ages, the present book is concerned essentially with children in the age and grade ranges which comprise the elementary school. These ranges are considered to be from approximately age five to approximately age twelve and grade levels from kindergarten to grade six. The following scale shows the approximate ages of children at the various grade levels.

Grade	*Age*
Kindergarten	5 to 6 years
First Grade	6 to 7 years
Second Grade	7 to 8 years
Third Grade	8 to 9 years
Fourth Grade	9 to 10 years
Fifth Grade	10 to 11 years
Sixth Grade	11 to 12 years

If one were to analyze the various statements of the purpose of elementary education, which have been made by responsible educational agencies and groups, it would be a relatively easy matter to identify a constantly emerging pattern. These statements through the years have gradually evolved into a more or less general agreement among present-day childhood educational leaders that the goal of elementary education is to stimulate and guide the *development* of an individual so that he or she will function in life activities involving vocation, citizenship, and enriched leisure; and, further, so that he or she will possess as high a level of

---

[1]Good, Carter, *Dictionary of Education*, 2nd ed, New York, 1959, p. 167.

3

physical, social, emotional, and intellectual well-being as his or her individual capacity will permit. More succinctly stated, the purpose of elementary education in our modern society should be in the direction of *total development* of the child during the formative years, which include kindergarten through grade six.

If it is a valid assumption that the purpose of elementary education is to attempt to insure total development of children, then it is incumbent upon teachers, parents, and other adults who deal in some way with children to explore the developmental processes as they relate to education.

When it is considered that the development of children brings about needs, and that these needs must be met satisfactorily, the importance of an understanding of development is readily discerned. When an understanding of the various aspects of developments is accomplished, one is then in a better position to provide improved procedures for meeting the needs of each individual child. This implies that we might well be guided by what could be called a developmental philosophy if we are to meet with any degree of success in our dealings with children.

GENERAL CHARACTERISTICS OF ELEMENTARY SCHOOL CHILDREN

As elementary, school-age children progress through the various stages of development, certain distinguishing characteristics can be identified that suggest implications for the developmental process. (The characteristics given here are general in nature, and they will be delineated in detail in subsequent chapters.)

During the range of age levels from five through seven, children begin their formal education. In our culture a child leaves the home for a part of the day to take his or her place in school with children of approximately the same chronological age. Not only are these children taking an important step toward becoming increasingly more independent and self-reliant, but as they learn they move from being a highly self-centered individual to becoming more socialized members of the group.

This age is ordinarily characterized by a certain lack of motor coordination, because the small muscles of the hands and fingers are not as well developed as the large muscles of the arms and legs. Thus, as children start their formal education, they need to use large crayons or pencils as one means of expressing themselves. The urge to action is expressed through movement since the child lives in a movement world, so to speak. Children at these age levels thrive on vigorous activity. They develop as they climb, run, jump, hop, skip, or keep time to music. An important physical aspect at this level is that the eyeball is increasing in size, and the eye muscles are developing. This factor is an important determinant in the child's readiness to see and read small print, and, thus, it involves a sequence from large print on charts to primer type in preprimers and primers.

Even though children have a relatively short attention span, they are extremely curious about the environment. At this state the teacher can capitalize upon the child's urge to learn by providing opportunities to gain information from first-hand experiences through the use of the senses. The child sees, hears, smells, feels, tastes, and moves in order to learn.

The age range from eight to ten is the period that usually marks the time spent in third and fourth grades. Children now have a wider range of interests and a longer attention span. While strongly individualistic, the child is working more from a position in a group. Organized games should afford opportunities for developing and practicing skills in good leadership and followership as well as body control, strength, and endurance. Small muscles are developing, manipulative skills are increasing, and muscular coordination is improving. The eyes have developed to a point where many children can and do read more widely. The child is more capable of getting information from books and is beginning to learn more through vicarious experience. This is the stage in development when skills of communication (listening, speaking, reading, and writing) and the number system are needed to deal with situations both in and out of school.

During the ages of ten through twelve most children complete the fifth and sixth grades. This is a period of transition for most as they go from childhood into the pre-adolescent periods of their development. They may show concern over bodily changes and are sometimes self-conscious about appearance. At this range of age levels, children tend to differ widely in physical maturation and emotional stability. Greater deviations in development can be noticed within the sex groups than between them. Rate of physical growth can be rapid, sometimes showing itself in poor posture and restlessness. It is essential to recognize at this level that prestige among peers is likely to be more important than adult approval. During this period, the child is ready for a higher level of intellectual skills that involve reasoning, discerning fact from opinion, noting cause-and-effect relationships, drawing conclusions, and using various references to locate and compare validity of information. The child is beginning to show more proficiency in expression through oral and written communication.

Thus, during the years of kindergarten through completion of sixth grade, the child develops (1) socially, from a self-centered individual to a participating member of the group; (2) emotionally, from a state manifesting anger outbursts to a higher degree of self-control; (3) physically, from childhood to the brink of adolescence, and (4) intellectually, from learning by first-hand experiences to learning from technical and specialized resources.

If the child is to be educated as a growing organism, aspects of development need the utmost consideration in planning and guiding learning experiences that will be most profitable for the child at a particular stage of development.

FORMS OF DEVELOPMENT

As mentioned, the major forms of development are the physical, social, emotional, and intellectual aspects. Of course, there are other forms of development, but perhaps they can be subclassified under one of the above areas. For example, *motor development,* which is a progressive change in motor performance can be considered a part of the broader aspect of *physical development.* (Chapter 3 considers motor development in detail.) In addition, *moral development,* which is concerned with the capacity of the individual to distinguish between standards of right and wrong could be considered as a dimension of the broader aspect of *social development.* This is to say that moral development involving achievement in ability to determine right from wrong is influential in the individual's social behavior.

It seems appropriate at this point to comment on other terminology that is sometimes used by educators to describe forms of development. Reference is made to what are ordinarily considered as the *learning domains.* These consist of the *affective* domain, the *cognitive* domain, and the *psychomotor* domain. Some writers refer to these as forms of development, i.e., affective development, cognitive development, and psychomotor development.

In this frame of reference, affective development is ordinarily thought of as being concerned with "appreciation," and is sometimes referred to as a combination of social-emotional development. Cognitive development in this context means knowledge or understanding. Psychomotor development involves learning to move with control and efficiency, or more simply stated, skill in movement.

A CONCEPT OF *TOTAL* CHILD DEVELOPMENT

A great deal of clinical and experimental evidence indicates that a human being must be considered as a whole and not a collection of parts. This means that a child is a unified individual or what is more popularly known as the *whole* child.

Total development is "one thing" comprising the various major forms of development. All of these components—physical, social, emotional, and intellectual—are highly interrelated and interdependent. All are of importance to well-being. The condition of any one of these forms of development affects other forms to a degree and, thus, total development as a whole. When a nervous child stutters or becomes nauseated, a mental state is not necessarily causing a physical symptom. On the contrary, a pressure imposed upon the child causes a series of reactions, which include thought, verbalization, digestive processes, and muscular function. It is not always necessarily true that the mind causes the body to become upset; the total organism is upset by a particular situation and reflects its upset in several ways, including disturbance in thought, feeling, and bodily processes. The whole child responds in interaction with the social and physical environment, and as the child is affected by the environment, he or she in turn has an effect upon it.

However, because of long tradition during which physical development *or* intellectual development, rather than physical *and* intellectual development, has been glorified, we oftentimes are still accustomed to dividing the two in our thinking. The result may be that we sometimes pull human beings apart with this kind of thinking.

Traditional attitudes that tended to separate the mind and body could lead to unbalanced development of the child with respect to mind and body and/or social adjustment. What is more important is that we fail to utilize the strengths of one to serve the needs of the other.

The foregoing statements have attempted to point out rather forcefully the idea that the identified components of total development comprise the unified individual. The fact that each of these aspects might well be considered as a separate entity should also be taken into account. As such, each aspect should warrant a separate discussion. This appears extremely important if one is to understand fully the place of each aspect as an integral part of total development. The following discussions of the physical, social, emotional, and intellectual aspects of development as they relate to children should be viewed in this general frame of reference.

Physical Development

One point of departure in discussing physical development could be to state that "everybody has a body." Some are short, some are tall, some are lean, and some are fat. Children come in different sizes, but all of them are born with certain capacities that are influenced by the environment.

It might be said of the child that he "is" his body. It is something that he can see. It is his base of operation. The other components of total development — social, emotional, and intellectual — are somewhat vague where the child is concerned. Although these are manifested in various ways, children do not always see them as they do the physical aspect. Consequently, it becomes important that a child be helped early in life to gain control over the physical aspect, or what is known as *basic body control*. The ability to do this, of course, will vary from one child to another. It will likely depend upon the status of *physical fitness* of the child. The broad areas of physical fitness can be broken down into certain components, and it is important that individuals achieve to the best of their natural ability with these components. Although there is not complete agreement on these components of physical fitness, the general consensus is that they consist of muscular strength, endurance, and power; circulatory-respiratory endurance; agility; speed; flexibility; balance; and coordination.

The components of physical fitness can be measured by calibrated instruments, such as measurements of muscular strength. Moreover, we can tell how tall a child is or how heavy he or she is at any stage of his or her development. In addition, other accurate data can be derived with assessments of blood pressure, blood counts, urinalysis, and the like.

Social Development

Human beings are social beings. They work together for the benefit of society. They have fought together in time of national emergencies in order to preserve the kind of society they believe in. While all this may be true, the social aspect is still quite vague and confusing, particularly where children are concerned.

It was a relatively easy matter to identify certain components of physical fitness such as strength, endurance, and the like. However, this does not necessarily hold true for the social aspect. The components for physical fitness are the same for children as for adults. On the other hand, the components of social fitness for children may be different from the components of social fitness for adults. By some adult standards children might be considered as social misfits because certain behavior of children might not be socially acceptable to some adults.

To the chagrin of some adults, young children are uninhibited in their social development. In this regard we need to be concerned with social maturity as it pertains to the growing and ever-changing child. This is to say that we need to give consideration to certain characteristics of social maturity and how well they are dealt with at the different stages of child development.

Perhaps adults should ask themselves such questions as: Are we helping children to become self-reliant by giving them independence at the proper time? Are we helping them to be outgoing and interested in others as well as themselves? Are we helping them to know how to satisfy their own needs in a socially desirable way? Are we helping them to develop a wholesome attitude toward themselves and others?

Emotional Development

In considering the subject of emotion we are confronted with the fact that for many years it has been a difficult concept to define, and, in addition, there have been many changing ideas and theories in the study of emotion. A few general statements relative to the nature of emotion will appear here, and Chapter 5 will deal with emotional development in some detail.

As will be seen in Chapter 5, there are pleasant emotions and those that are unpleasant. For example, joy could be considered as pleasant emotional experience, while fear would be an unpleasant one. It is interesting to note that a good proportion of the literature is devoted to emotions that are unpleasant. It has been found that in books on psychology much more space is given to such emotional patterns as fear, hate, and guilt than to such pleasant emotions as love, sympathy, and contentment.

Generally speaking, the pleasantness or unpleasantness of an emotion seems to be determined by its strength or intensity, by the nature of the situation arousing it, and by the way a child perceives or interprets the situation. The emotions of young children tend to be more intense than those of adults. If adults are not aware of this aspect of child behavior, they will not be likely to understand why a child reacts rather violently to a situation that to them seems somewhat insignificant. The fact that different children will react differently to the same type of situation also should be taken into account. For example, something that might anger one child might have a rather passive influence on another.

Intellectual Development

The word "intelligence" is derived from the Latin word *intellectus,* which literally means the "power of knowing." Intelligence has been defined in many ways. One general description of it is *the capacity to learn or understand.*

Children possess various degrees of intelligence, and most fall within a range of what is called "Normal" intelligence. In dealing with this we should perhaps give attention to what might be called *intellectual fitness.* However, this is difficult to do. Because of the somewhat vague nature of intelligence, it is practically impossible to identify specific components of it. Thus, we need to view intellectual fitness in a somewhat different manner.

For purposes of this discussion we will consider intellectual fitness from two different, but closely related points of view; first, from a standpoint of intellectual needs, and second, from a standpoint of how certain things influence intelligence. It might be said that if the child's intellectual needs are being met, then perhaps we could also say that he or she is intellectually fit. From the second point of view, if we know how certain things influence intelligence then we might understand better how to contribute to intellectual fitness by improving upon some of these factors.

There appears to be some rather general agreement with regard to the intellectual needs of children. Among others, these needs include (1) a need for challenging experiences at the child's level of ability, (2) a need for intellectually successful and satisfying experiences, and (3) a need for the opportunity to participate in creative experiences instead of always having to conform. Some of the factors that tend to influence intelligence are (1) health and physical condition, (2) emotional disturbance, and (3) certain social and economic factors. When teachers, parents, and other adults have a realization of intellectual needs and factors influencing intelligence, perhaps then they will be able to deal more satisfactorily with children in helping them in their intellectual pursuits.

MEETING THE NEEDS OF CHILDREN

In discussing needs of children it is important to consider their *interests* as well. Although needs and interests of children are closely related and highly interdependent, there are certain important differences that need to be taken into account.

Needs of children, particularly those of an individual nature, are likely to be innate. On the other hand, interests may be acquired as products of the environment. It is possible that a child may demonstrate an interest in a certain unsafe practice that is obviously not in accord with his needs at a certain age level. The two year old may be interested in running into the street, but this practice might result in injury. Acquiring a particular interest because of environmental conditions is further illustrated in the case of children coming from families that are superstitious about certain kinds of foods or certain foods eaten in combination. In such cases, acquiring such an interest from other family members might build up a lifetime resistance to a certain kind of food that might be very nutritious and beneficial to the child's physical needs.

One of the most important aspects is that of obtaining a proper balance between needs and interests. However, arriving at a suitable ratio between needs and interests is not an easy task. Although we should undoubtedly think first in terms of meeting the child's needs, we must also consider his interests. A general principle by which we might be guided is that the *lower* the age level of children, the more we should take the responsibility for meeting their needs. This is based on the obvious assumption that the younger the child, the less experience he or she has had, and consequently there is less opportunity to develop certain interests. In other words, a lack of interest at an early age level might possibly be synonymous with ignorance.

Classification of Needs

It is a well-known fact that children's needs have been classified in many ways. However, it should be borne in mind that any classification of needs is usually an arbitrary one made for a specific purpose. For example, when one speaks of biological needs and psychological needs it should be understood that each of these, although classified separately, are interdependent. The classification of needs that we will use will be the same as for the forms of development, that is, physical, social, emotional, and intellectual. (In subsequent chapters we will get into these needs in greater detail.)

HELPING CHILDREN UNDERSTAND ABOUT THEIR OWN DEVELOPMENT

Among the various other struggles a child encounters in the process of developing is that of gaining an understanding of *self.* It is the purpose of this section of the chapter to provide information that will help teachers, parents, and other adults become more successful in their efforts to aid children in the process of self-realization, and thus, a better understanding of their own development.

In recent years there has been an increasing sentiment among young men and women of high school and college age that they have a need to *find* themselves. This should fortify the notion that one of the most important aspects of the "growing up" years is that children develop an understanding of themselves. This can be accomplished to some extent when adults improve upon their knowledge about children and, perhaps more important, being prepared to use this knowledge with children as they grow and develop.

As much as possible, teachers and parents should provide an environment in the school and home that is a stable sanctuary that the child knows will be there when needed. Children need to be accepted for themselves, with their own unique abilities and limitations. They need to be permitted to grow and learn at their own rate and in their own way—and not be made to feel inadequate in developing and learning even though they may not conform themselves to some standard or "norm." They need to identify themselves as distinct individuals, and their uniqueness is deserving of respect. As children mature, they should have the opportunity to assume independence and responsibilities that are commensurate with their age and abilities.

Children require control and discipline that is consistent, reasonable, and understandable to them. A few clear and simple rules are usually entirely adequate and tend to give children a feeling of security, in that they know what they can do and what they cannot do. Therefore, it may be said that children need defined limits to prevent them from destructive behavior and perhaps from even destroying themselves. It is important to emphasize that consistency in all aspects of the environment is very important. For example, acts for which they are ignored, praised, or punished should not vary from time to time. If they do, children are likely to become confused and their adjustment made more difficult. Similarly, expression of love should not be spasmodic, nor should the threat of withdrawal of love be used as an occasional weapon to control behavior.

Modern standard dictionaries ordinarily list almost 500 hyphenated words beginning with *self*—from *self*-abandonment to *self*-worth. The discussion here is going to be concerned with *self*-image, or how one conceives oneself or one's role. Reflecting back to the comments on physical development, recall the suggestion that where the child is concerned, *he is his body;* that is, he is essentially concerned with his *physical self.* It is something he can see and is much more meaningful to him than his social, emotional or intellectual *self.* This being the case, attention is now turned to what will be called *body image,* which is the child's picture of his bodily person and his abilities. It has been clearly demonstrated that when teachers help children improve upon body image, then a basic understanding of the broader aspect of self will more likely be established.

Determining Deficiencies in Body Image

One of the first steps is to determine if a child has problems with body image. In this regard, it is doubtful that there is any absolutely foolproof method of detecting problems of body image in children. The reason for this is that many mannerisms said to be indicative of body image problems can also be the same as for other deficiencies. Nevertheless, teachers should be on the alert to certain possible deficiencies.

Generally speaking, there are two ways in which deficiencies concerned with body image can be detected, at least in part, by observing certain behaviors. And, second, there are some relatively simple diagnostic techniques that can be used to determine such deficiencies. The following generalized list contains examples of both of these possibilities and is submitted to assist the reader in this particular regard.

1. One technique often used to diagnose possible problems of body image is to have children make a drawing of themselves. The primary reason for this is to see if certain parts of the body are *not* included in the drawing. The personal experience of one of the authors as a Certified Binet Intelligence Test Examiner has revealed

possibilities for such a diagnosis in the test item involving *picture completion.* In this test item a partial drawing of a "man" is provided for the child to complete. Since the child's interest in drawing a man dates from his earliest attempts to represent things symbolically, it is possible, through typical drawings by young children, to trace certain characteristic stages of perceptual development. It has also been found in recent years that the procedure of drawing a picture of himself assists in helping to detect if there is a lack of body image.

2. Sometimes, the child with a lack of body image may manifest tenseness in movements. At the same time, he may be unsure of his movements as he attempts to move the body segments.

3. If the child is instructed to move a body part such as placing one foot forward, he may direct his attention to the body part before making the movement. Or he may look at another child to observe the movement before he attempts to make the movement himself. This could also possibly be due to poor processing of the input (auditory or visual stimulus) provided for the movement.

4. When instructed to use one body part (arm), he may also move the corresponding body part (other arm) when it is not necessary. For example, he may be asked to swing the right arm and he may also start swinging the left arm simultaneously.

5. In such activities as catching an object, the child may turn toward the object when this is not necessary. For example, when a bean-bag thrown to him approaches close to the child, he may move forward with either side of the body rather than trying to retrieve the beanbag with his hands while both feet remain stationary.

Improving Upon Body Image

In general, it might be said that when a child is given the opportunity to use his body freely in enjoyable movement, an increase in body image occurs. More specifically, there are activities that can be used in helping children identify and understand the use of various body parts, as well as the relationship of these parts.

Over the years a number of experiments have been conducted in an attempt to determine the effect of participation in certain body-movement activities on body image. The following is an example of this approach, utilizing the game *Busy Bee.*

In this game, the children are in pairs facing each other and dispersed around the activity area. One child who is the *caller* is in the center of the area. This child makes calls, such as "shoulder to shoulder," "toe to toe," or "hand to hand." (In the early stages of the game, it might be a good idea for the teacher to do the calling.) As the calls are made, the paired children go through the appropriate motions with their partners. After a few calls, the caller will shout, "Busy Bee!" This is the signal for every child to get a new partner, including the caller. The child who does not get a partner can name the new caller.

This game has been experimented with in the following manner: As the children played the game, the teacher made them aware of the location of various parts of the body in order to develop the concept of full-body image. Before the game was played, the children were asked to draw a picture of themselves. Many did not know how to begin, and others omitted some of the major limbs in their drawings. After playing Busy Bee, the children were asked again to draw a picture of themselves. This time they were more successful. All of the drawings had bodies, heads, arms, and legs. Some of them had hands, feet, eyes, and ears. A few even had teeth and hair.

Some activities are concerned with the process of identification in terms of certain characteristics that children might possess. The following simulated teaching-learning situation shows how a teacher might originally introduce the concept of body-image using the game *Have You Seen My Sheep?*

The players may stand or be seated in a circle. One player is selected to be *It* to act as a "farmer" or a "shepherd." He walks around the outside of the circle, stops behind one of the children, and asks, "Have you seen my sheep?" The child responds by asking, "What does your sheep look like?" *It* then describes another player in the circle while the second child tries to determine who is being described. As soon as he finds out from the description who the described player is, he chases that individual around the outside of the circle, trying to tag him before he can run around the circle and return to his place. If the player is tagged, he becomes *It*. If he is not tagged, the chaser is *It* and the game is repeated. The original *It* does not take part in this chase, but steps into the circle in the space vacated by the chaser. If the game is played in the classroom, the children may sit in their seats. The person described runs for safety to a designated empty seat. The person who was *It* goes back to his own seat.

Teacher: In reading we have learned that some words look alike, and some have small differences. Each boy and girl looks like some other one in one way or another, but each has an individual look that makes him or her different from anyone else. Do you think you would recognize yourself if I described you?

Child: If you said a boy with red hair, I would know who it is.

Teacher: That would be easy because Frank is the only boy with red hair in our class. Do you think you could describe someone else so that we could recognize him or her?

Child: Can I try it first?

Teacher: We can play a game where we can see if we can describe others and also recognize ourselves when we are described. The game is called "Have You Seen My Sheep?" Will you make a circle? Fred, let's make believe you are a farmer and that you have lost one of your sheep. You will walk around the circle and tap someone on the back. Then you will say to that person, "Have you seen my sheep?" The person that you tap will ask, "What does your sheep look like?" You will then tell the person what your sheep looks like, describing one of the children in the circle. When the one you tapped guesses the person in the circle you are describing, he chases him around the circle and tries to tag him before he can return to his place. Does everyone understand how to play the game?

Child: What happens if you get caught?

Child: Is the sheep *It?*

Teacher: Yes, the sheep then becomes the farmer and the game is played again.

(The children play the game and the teacher evaluates it with them)

Teacher: George, you seemed to be having a good time. What did you like about the game?

Child: I like to be chased, and I didn't get caught.

Teacher: How can we help each other in this game?

Child: We have to listen when someone is talking.

Teacher: We learned how to play a new game that was fun. What else did we learn?

Child: We learned that some of us look alike in some ways.

Child: And we learned that we are different in some ways.

Child: We used color words and we used the names of kinds of clothes that kids wear.

Teacher: How were you able to tell who the sheep was?

Child: By listening to the person tell about him.

Teacher: What did those of you who were farmers find that you had to do in telling about the sheep? What do you think, Jane?

Child: I had to be able to tell Mary exactly what George looked like. I had to explain it to her so she could tell who I was talking about.

Teacher: Fine! You seemed to have fun and also you saw the need for being able to explain something to someone else.

Among the following activities will be found those that can be used for diagnosis for lack of body image, body-image improvement, evaluation of body-image status, or various combinations of these factors. Some of the activities are age-old, while others have been developed for specific conditions.

Come with Me

Several children form a circle, with one child outside the circle. The child outside the circle walks around it, taps another child and says, "Come with me." The child tapped falls in behind the first child and they continue walking around the circle. The second child taps a child and says "Come with me." This continues until several children have been tapped. At a given point the first child calls out, "Go home!" On this signal all the children try to get back to their original place in the circle. The first child also tries to get into one of these places. There will be one child left out. He can be the first child for the next game.

In the early stages of this game the teacher should call out where each child is to be tapped. For example, "on the arm," "on the leg," etc. After awhile, the child doing the tapping can call out where he is going to tap the child. The teacher can observe if children are tapped in the proper place.

Mirrors

One child is selected as the leader and stands in front of a line of children. This child goes through a variety of different movements and the children in the line try to do exactly the same thing; that is, they act as mirrors. The leader should be changed frequently.

In this activity, the children become aware of different body parts and movements as the child in front makes the various movements. The teacher should be alert to see how well and how quickly the children are able to do the movements that the child leader makes.

Change Circles

Several circles are drawn on the floor or outdoor activity area with one less circle than the number of participants. The one child who does not have a circle can be *IT* and stands in the middle of the area. The teacher calls out signals in the form of body parts. For example, such calls could include: "hands on knees," "hand on head," "right hand on left foot," and so on. After a time, the teacher calls out, "Change circles!" whereupon all the children try to get into a different circle while the child who is *IT* tries to find a circle. The child who does not find a circle can be *IT* or a new person can be chosen to be *IT.*

The teacher should observe closely to see how the children react to the calls and whether or not they are looking at the other children for clues. As times goes on and the children become more familiar with body parts, more complicated calls can be made.

Body Tag

In this game one child is selected to be *IT.* He chases the other children and attempts to tag one of them. If he is successful, the child tagged can become *IT.* If *IT* does not succeed within a reasonable amount of time, a new *IT* can be selected. In order to be officially tagged, a specific part of the body must be tagged by *IT.* Thus, the game could be shoulder tag, arm tag, or leg tag as desired.

The teacher observes the child to see whether or not he tags the correct body part. To add more interest to the activity, the teacher can call out the part of the body to be tagged during each session of the game.

These are just a few of the possibilities for improving upon body image and, thus, an understanding of self. Creative teachers should be able to think of numerous others that could satisfy this purpose. The above activities as well as many similar ones have been field tested with large numbers of children and have been found to be very successful in improving their body image.

Chapter 2

PHYSICAL DEVELOPMENT

Physical development is concerned with the child's physical ability to function at an increasingly higher level. For example, a stage of development in the infant is from creeping to crawling. This is later followed by the developmental stage of walking when the child moves to an upright position and begins to move over the surface area by putting one foot in front of the other.

PHYSICAL NEEDS OF CHILDREN

Needs of a physical nature are concerned with the basic anatomical structure and basic physiological function of the human organism. Included here, of course, are the need for food, rest, and activity, and proper care of the eyes, ears, teeth, and the like. Physical needs are also concerned with such factors as strength, endurance, agility, flexibility, and balance as elements of physical fitness of the organism.

The physical needs are reflected in the physical developmental characteristics of growing children. Many such characteristics are identified in the following lists of the different age levels.

This list of physical characteristics, as well as the lists of social, emotional, and intellectual characteristics, which will appear in subsequent chapters, have been developed through a documentary analysis of over a score of sources that have appeared in the literature in recent years. It should be understood that these characteristics are suggestive of the behavior patterns of the so-called normal child. This implies that if a child does not conform to these characteristics, it should not be interpreted to mean that he or she is seriously deviating from the normal. In other words, it should be recognized that each child progresses at his or her own rate and that there will be much overlapping of the characteristics for each of the age levels.

Five-Year-Old Children

1. Boys' height, 42 to 46 inches; weight, 38 to 49 pounds; girls' height, 42 to 46 inches; weight, 36 to 48 pounds.
2. May grow two or three inches and gain from three to six pounds during the year.
3. Girls may be about a year ahead of boys in physiological development.
4. Beginning to have better control of body.
5. The large muscles are better developed than the small muscles that control the fingers and hands.
6. Usually determined whether he or she will be right- or left-handed.
7. Eye and hand coordination is not complete.
8. May have farsighted vision.
9. Vigorous and noisy, but activity appears to have definite direction.
10. Tires easily and needs plenty of rest.

Six-Year-Old Children

1. Boys' height, 44 to 48 inches; weight, 41 to 54 pounds; girls' height, 43 to 48 inches; weight, 40 to 53 pounds.
2. Growth is gradual in weight and height.
3. Good supply of energy.
4. Marked activity urge absorbs him in running, jumping, chasing, and dodging games.
5. Muscular control becoming more effective with large objects.
6. There is a noticeable change in the eye-hand behavior.
7. Legs lengthening rapidly.
8. Big muscles crave activity.

Seven-Year-Old Children

1. Boys' height, 46 to 51 inches; weight, 45 to 60 pounds; girls' height, 46 to 50 inches; weight, 44 to 59 pounds.
2. Big muscle activity predominates in interest and value.
3. More improvement in eye-hand coordination.
4. May grow two or three inches and gain three to five pounds in weight during the year.
5. Tires easily and shows fatigue in the afternoon.
6. Has slow reaction time.

7. Heart and lungs are smallest in proportion to body size.
8. General health may be precarious, with susceptibility to disease high and resistance low.
9. Endurance is relatively low.
10. Coordination is improving with throwing, and catching becoming more accurate.
11. Whole-body movements are under better control.
12. Small accessory muscles developing.
13. Displays amazing amounts of vitality.

Eight-Year-Old Children

1. Boys' height, 48 to 53 inches; weight, 49 to 70 pounds; girls' height, 48 to 52 inches; weight, 47 to 66 pounds.
2. Interested in games requiring coordination of small muscles.
3. Arms are lengthening and hands are growing larger.
4. Eyes can accommodate more easily.
5. Some develop poor posture.
6. Accidents appear to occur more frequently at this age.
7. Appreciates correct skill performance.

Nine-Year-Old Children

1. Boys' height, 50 to 55 inches; weight, 55 to 74 pounds; girls' height, 50 to 54 inches; weight, 52 to 74 pounds.
2. Increasing strength in arms, hands, and fingers.
3. Endurance improving.
4. Needs and enjoys much activity; boys like to shout, wrestle, and tussle with each other.
5. A few girls near puberty.
6. Girls gaining growth maturity up to two years over boys.
7. Girls enjoy active group games, but are usually less noisy and less full of spontaneous energy than boys.
8. Likely to slouch and assume unusual postures.
9. Eyes are much better developed and are able to accommodate to close work with less strain.
10. May tend to overexercise.
11. Sex differences appear in recreational activities.
12. Interested in own body and wants to have questions answered.

Ten-Year-Old Children

1. Boys' height, 52 to 57 inches; weight, 59 to 82 pounds; girls' height, 52 to 57 inches; weight, 57 to 83 pounds.
2. Individuality is well-defined, and insights are more mature.
3. Stability in growth rate and stability of physiological processes.
4. Physically active and likes to rush around and be busy.
5. Before the onset of puberty there is usually a resting period or plateau, during which the boy or girl does not appear to gain in either height or weight.
6. Interested in the development of more skills.
7. Reaction time is improving.
8. Muscular strength does not seem to keep pace with growth.
9. Refining and elaborating skill in the use of small muscles.

Eleven-Year-Old Children

1. Boys' height, 53 to 58 inches; weight 64 to 91 pounds; girls' height, 53 to 59 inches; weight 64 to 95 pounds.
2. Marked changes in muscle system causing awkwardness and habits sometimes distressing to the child.
3. Shows fatigue more easily.
4. Some girls and a few boys suddenly show rapid growth and evidence of the approach of adolescence.
5. On the average, girls may be taller and heavier than boys.
6. Uneven growth of different parts of the body.
7. Rapid growth may result in laziness of the lateral type of child and fatigue and irritability in the linear type.
8. Willing to work hard at acquiring physical skills, and emphasis is on excellence of performance of physical feats.
9. Boys are more active and rough in games than girls.
10. Eye-hand coordination is well developed.
11. Bodily growth is more rapid than heart growth, and lungs are not fully developed.
12. Boys develop greater power in shoulder girdle muscles.

Twelve-Year-Old Children

1. Boys' height, 55 to 61 inches; weight, 70 to 101 pounds; girls' height, 56 to 72 inches; weight 72 to 107 pounds.

2. Becoming more skillful in the use of small muscles.
3. May be relatively little body change in some cases.
4. Ten hours of sleep is considered average.
5. Heart rate at rest is between 80 and 90.

It is perhaps appropriate to comment on the ranges of height and weight given here. These heights and weights are what might be called a range within a range, and are computed means or averages within larger ranges. In other words, some children at a given age level could possibly weigh much more or less and be much taller or shorter than the ranges indicate. To illustrate how wide a range can be, one study of a large number of children showed that eleven-year-old girls ranged in weight from 45 to 180 pounds.

GUIDELINES FOR PHYSICAL DEVELOPMENT

It is important to set forth some guidelines for physical development if we are to meet with any degree of success in our attempts to provide for such physical development of children. The reason for this is to assure, at least to some extent, that our efforts in attaining optimum physical development will be based upon a scientific approach. These guidelines might well take the form of valid *concepts of physical development.* This approach enables us to give serious consideration to what is known about how children grow and develop. Thus, we can select experiences that are compatible with the physical developmental process. The following list of concepts of physical development should be viewed in this general frame of reference.

1. *Physical development and change is continuous, orderly, progressive, and differentiated.* In the early years children's experiences might well be characterized by large muscle activities. As the child develops, more difficult types of skills and activities can be introduced so that experiences progress in a way that is compatible with the child's development.

2. *Physical development is controlled by both heredity and environment.* Programs should be planned in such a way as to contribute to the innate capacities of each child. Attempts should be made to establish an environmental climate where all children have an equal opportunity for wholesome participation.

3. *Differences in physical development occur at each age level.* This implies that there should be a wide variety of activities to meet the needs

of children at various developmental levels. While gearing activities to meet the needs of a particular group of children, attempts should also be made to provide for individual differences of children within the group.

4. *Needs of a physical nature must be satisfied if a child is to function effectively.* Experiences should be planned to provide an adequate activity yield. Programs should be vigorous enough to meet the physical needs of children and, at the same time, motivating enough so that they will desire to perpetuate such experiences outside of school.

5. *Various parts of the body develop at different rates and at different ages.* Undue strain to the point of excessive fatigue should be avoided in activities. Teachers should be aware of fatigue symptoms so that children are not likely to go beyond their physical capacity. The use of large muscles should predominate activities, at least at the primary level.

6. *The individual's own growth pattern will vary from that of others both as to time and rate.* It might be well to compare a child's performance with his or her own previous achievements rather than that of classmates. It should be recognized that we should not expect the same standards of performance from all children in any given activity due to individual differences.

7. *There are early maturers and late maturers.* This concept suggests the importance of proper grouping of children. The teacher should be aware as to when it will be most profitable to classify children either homogeneously or heterogeneously for certain kinds of experiences.

8. *The level of physical maturation of the child often has a significant effect on learning.* Very young children should not be expected to achieve beyond their ability levels.

9. *Physical differences may have a marked effect on personality.* A variety of experiences should be provided in an effort to give each child a chance to find some successful physical achievement within his or her own physical capacity. The teacher should set the example for children to learn to be respectful of physical differences by helping children to use their particular body type in the most advantageous way.

When programs for children are planned and implemented on the basis of what is known about how they grow and develop, there is a greater likelihood that worthwhile contributions can be made to physical development. Adherence to valid concepts of physical development is one of the best ways of accomplishing this goal.

CONTRIBUTIONS SCHOOL PROGRAMS MAKE TO PHYSICAL DEVELOPMENT

Perhaps the part of the school curriculum best suited to contributing to physical development of children is found in the physical education program. In this regard, sometime ago in what has become a classic report, G. Lawrence Rarick, who was for many years physical education's leading spokesperson on physical growth and development of children, called attention to some results of research that bear upon physical activity as it relates to physical development.[1] The following is a summary of the highlights of this report:

1. There is little or no evidence that planned physical activity experiences have an influence on the growth in height of children.

2. There is sufficient information on exercise and muscle growth to provide us with general guidelines in designing physical activity programs if our purpose is to favorably affect general growth and muscular development without overdoing it.

3. One of the most striking effects of vigorous activity during the growing years is its influence upon the child's body composition, that is, the relative amount of lean, fat-free body mass. Some studies have shown that boys included in a vigorous regular physical activity program, as compared to inactive boys, substantially increased their lean body mass at the expense of fat.

4. There is general agreement that moderate stress in the form of vigorous exercise is a positive force in building sturdy bones. However, the difficulty involved in the assessment of the exact influence of physical activity on bone growth makes it almost impossible to evaluate the effect of planned physical activity programs on this aspect of growth.

5. The specific effect of school physical activity programs on physical development of children shows that little or no solid data collected on a longitudinal basis exists to support the hypothesis made by many physical educators. Studies made on a short-range basis have produced varying and sometimes conflicting results.

In summarizing research in this general area, it is suggested that while we know that the stimulus of physical activity is essential to insure the normal physical growth and physiological development of children, we

---

[1]Rarick, G. Lawrence, Effects of physical activity on the growth and development of children, *The Academy Papers*, No. 8, American Academy of Physical Education, Anaheim, California, March 27–28, 1974.

do not know the amount or intensity that is necessary. In addition, its effects most assuredly vary within the individual from one period of development to another and differ widely among individuals. And, further, the importance of physical activity in the development of children goes beyond its effect on structural and morphological growth, for its true significance rests on what it does for the child as a functioning, responding being. Finally, without a sound structural organic base, unfortunate limitations are almost certain to be imposed on what might have been a strong, vigorous, and healthy child.

EVALUATING CONTRIBUTIONS OF PHYSICAL EDUCATION TO PHYSICAL DEVELOPMENT

Some attempt should be made to assess the potential contribution made by those physical education experiences that are provided for children. One of the first steps in this direction is to consider the extent to which the physical education activities help to maintain a suitable level of physical fitness.

It determining whether or not physical education experiences are contributing to the child's physical fitness, consideration needs to be given to the identification of specific components comprising the broad aspect of physical fitness. We know that there is not complete agreement regarding the components of physical fitness. However, a general consensus suggests certain components to be basic, as follows:

1. *Muscular Strength.* This refers to the contraction power of the muscles. The strength of muscles is usually measured by dynometers or tensiometers, which record the amount of force particular muscle groups can apply in a single maximum effort. Man's existence and effectiveness depend upon his muscles. All movements of the body or any of its parts are impossible without action by muscles attached to the skeleton. Muscles perform vital functions of the body as well. The heart is a muscle; death occurs when it ceases to contract. Breathing, digestion, and elimination are impossible without muscular contractions. These vital muscular functions are influenced by exercising the skeletal muscles; the heart beats faster, the blood circulates through the body at a greater rate, breathing becomes deep and rapid, and perspiration breaks out on the surface of the skin.

2. *Muscular Endurance.* Muscular endurance is the ability of the muscles to perform work. Two variations of muscular endurance are

recognized: *isometric,* whereby a maximum static muscular contraction is held; *isotonic,* whereby the muscles continue to raise and lower a submaximal load, as in weight training or performing push-ups. In the isometric form, the muscles maintain a fixed length; in the isotonic form, they alternately shorten and lengthen. Muscular endurance must assume some muscular strength, however, there are distinctions between the two; muscle groups of the same strength may possess different degrees of endurance.

3. *Circulatory-Respiratory Endurance.* Circulatory-respiratory endurance is characterized by moderate contractions of large muscle groups for relatively long periods of time during which maximal adjustments of the circulatory-respiratory system to the activity are necessary, as in distance running and swimming. Obviously, strong and enduring muscles are needed. However, by themselves, they are not enough; they do not guarantee well-developed circulatory and respiratory functions.

In addition to the basic three above, other components of physical fitness to be considered are:

1. *Muscular Power:* ability to release maximum muscular force in the shortest time. Example—standing broad jump.

2. *Agility:* speed in changing direction, or body position. Example—dodging run.

3. *Speed:* rapidity with which successive movements of the same kind can be performed. Example—50-yard dash.

4. *Flexibility:* range of movements in a joint or a sequence of joints. Example—touch fingers to floor without bending knees.

5. *Balance:* ability to maintain position and equilibrium both in movement (dynamic balance) and while stationary (static balance). Example—walking on a line or balance beam (dynamic); standing on one foot (static).

6. *Coordination:* working together of the muscles and organs of the human body in the performance of a specific task. Example—throwing or catching an object.

Having an understanding of the above components of physical fitness should be extremely helpful in one's efforts to evaluate the extent to which certain physical education experiences contribute to the maintenance of a suitable level of physical fitness. In fact, in planning physical education experiences for children, certain questions may be raised in connection with the activities used to bring about these experiences.

1. Does the activity provide for contraction power of muscles (muscular strength)?
2. Are there opportunities in the activity for isometric and/or isotonic muscular activity (muscular endurance)?
3. Does the activity provide for moderate contraction of large muscles for specified periods of time (circulatory-respiratory endurance)?
4. Does the activity involve ability to release maximum muscular force in a short period of time (muscular power)?
5. Is there opportunity in the activity to utilize speed in changing direction (agility)?
6. Does the activity require rapidity with successive movements of the same kind (speed)?
7. Does the activity involve various degrees of bending at the joints (flexibility)?
8. Is the activity one that involves the ability to maintain position and equilibrium (balance)?
9. Is the activity concerned with the working together of the muscles and organs in specific task performance (coordination)?

Of course, it is not to be expected that all activities will involve all of the components of physical fitness. For example, while a dodgeball-type game may require various degrees of agility, it does not necessarily involve a great deal of muscular strength. However, it would be possible to select enough activities with sufficient balance of the components over a period of time so that activities as a group could contribute to the total physical fitness of the child.

It should also be clearly understood that there are limits to which we may wish to conduct activities that involve certain components of physical fitness. For instance, it is not likely that with very young children we would want to utilize too many activities involving circulatory-respiratory endurance. This, of course, presupposes that teachers will have a sufficient understanding of the growing human organism as well as an understanding of the traits and characteristics of children at the various age levels.

Not only should a teacher consider this approach in planning activities, but for purposes of value assessment after activities have been conducted. With this procedure, some judgment could be made with reference to how well a given activity attained a given purpose. It should be kept in mind that the extent to which an activity may contribute to any given component of physical fitness will likely be contingent upon a variety of factors. Included among such factors are the ability level of a given group of children; number of children in a group; general nature of the activity; difficulty in providing for individual differences; where the activity takes place; and above all, the teacher's input and behavior.

It should be obvious that any assessment made in connection with this approach is limited because of subjectivity. Nevertheless, teachers' judgments in such matters should contain a great deal of validity, provided, as mentioned previously, that they have a clear understanding of the growing organism and the traits and characteristics at the various age levels.

PHYSICAL ACTIVITY YIELD

Another approach in determining the extent to which physical education activities contribute to physical fitness is known as *physical activity yield*. This is concerned with the amount of time that a majority of the children are meaningfully active in a physical education class period. The term *majority* can have a range of from one more than half of the children to all of the children in a class. Generally, the majority of children is considered to be 80 percent of them. This would mean that there would be activity yield for the class if 24 out of a class of 30 children were meaningfully active. Meaningfully active is interpreted as the children being involved in activity, such as a game or dance, that has a specific purpose and objective. Many teachers tend to agree that in a successful 30-minute class period, 18 to 20 minutes should be devoted to the participation phase of the period. Some persons who have used the physical activity yield approach report a range of as low as six minutes to as high as 23 minutes of activity yield as defined above.

For purposes of illustration, versions of the two games *Squirrels in Trees* and *Hill Dill* are used here to help clarify use of the idea of physical activity yield.

Squirrels in Trees

With the exception of one player, the children are arranged in groups of three. Two of the players in each group face each other and hold hands, forming a "Hollow tree." The third player is a squirrel and stand between the other two in the hollow tree. The extra player—who is also a squirrel—stands near the center of the playing area. The extra player calls out "Change." On this signal, all squirrels attempt to get into a different hollow tree, and the extra squirrel also tries to find a tree. There will always be one squirrel left who does not have a tree. After playing for a time, the players are alternated so that all will have an opportunity to be a squirrel.

Hill Dill

Two parallel goal lines are established approximately 60 feet apart. One person is selected to be *IT* and stands midway between the two goal lines. The rest of the group is divided into two equal groups, with one group standing on one goal line and the other on the other goal line. *IT* tries to tag as many as he can while they are exchanging goals. All of those tagged become helpers, and the game continues in this manner until all but one have been tagged. This person is *IT* for the next game. The game is started each time by *IT* calling out, "Hill Dill run over the hill."

In Squirrels in Trees, it will be seen that at any one time only one-third of the children plus one are "meaningfully active," because the other two-thirds stand forming hollow trees. In contrast, the game Hill Dill theoretically provides for activity yield for all of the children. This example should not be interpreted to mean that one of these activities is necessarily better than the other. It simply means that one has a greater potential for activity yield.

All physical education activities should be used to provide for certain more or less specific experiences for children. All of the various aspects of development—social, emotional, and intellectual, as well as physical—need to be taken into account in planning for physical education experiences over the long range.

It should be interesting to note that while the game Squirrels in Trees tended to provide a relatively small amount of activity yield as described above, it nevertheless is a very popular activity. Incidentally, one of the authors analyzed 15 elementary school physical education books and found that this activity was recommended the greatest number of times of any game activity for first-grade children. The reader can speculate as to the reason for this. In a follow-up of a large number of elementary school physical education teachers, the same results were obtained. This could suggest that teachers to a large extent rely upon information provided in books for the kinds of activities they select for children.

The physical activity yield approach differs appreciably from the previously mentioned approach in that it is not as precise and definitive; that is, it provides only for a recognition of general physical activity engaged in by children and not for specific physical fitness components.

In any event, the important factor to consider is that some attempt be made to arrive at an evaluation of the extent to which physical education activities contribute to the physical development of children, especially since this is the curriculum area that should contribute the most to such development. This, of course, requires that each physical education activity be carefully analyzed for its possible potential contribution to physical development, along with how the activity should be conducted, so that the most desirable and worthwhile results will be obtained.

Chapter 3

MOTOR DEVELOPMENT

We mentioned previously that motor development means a progressive change in motor performance and that it can be considered a part of the broader aspect of physical development. As far as human motion is concerned the term *motor* pertains to a muscle, nerve, or center that effects or produces movement. That is, a nerve connecting with a muscle causes the impulse for motion known as *motor impulse*. The terms *motion* or *movement* simply mean a change in body position. The human organism interacts with its environment through changes in position of the body and/or its segments through movement.

One of the most important characteristics of life is movement. Whatever else they may involve, practically all of man's achievements are based upon his ability to move. Obviously, the very young child is not an intelligent being in the sense of abstract thinking, and he only gradually acquires the ability to deal with symbols and intellectualize his experiences in the course of his development. On the other hand, the child is a creature of movement and feeling. Any effort to educate the child must take this dominance of movement in the life of the child into account. For the young child, being able to move as effectively and efficiently as possible is directly related to the proficiency with which he or she will be able to perform the various fundamental motor skills.

LOCOMOTOR MOVEMENTS

Locomotor movements involve changes in body position which propel the body over the surface area with the impetus being given by the feet and legs. There are five basic types of these movements, namely, walking, running, leaping, jumping, and hopping, and three combination movements which are galloping, skipping, and sliding. The first five of these are performed with an even rhythm and the last three are done with an uneven rhythm. The term *locomotor skills*, an area to be discussed in

depth later in this chapter, is concerned with the proficiency of performance of these locomotor movements.

AXIAL MOVEMENTS

Axial movements, or nonlocomotor movements, refer to bending and
stretching and twisting and turning, and the like. As in the case of
locomotor skills, the skill performance of axial movements will be discussed
in an ensuing section of the chapter.

Axial movements are ordinarily performed with a part of the body
remaining as a fixed base to the surface area. However, they can be done
with parts of the body or the whole body in gross movement. For
example, twisting can be combined with a locomotor movement to avoid
being hit in a game such as dodge ball.

FACTORS INVOLVED IN MOVEMENT

Generally speaking, in every body movement the following factors
should be taken into account:

1. *Time.* Time is concerned with how long it takes to complete a
movement. For example, a movement can be slow and deliberate such as
a child attempting to create his own body movement to depict a falling
snowflake. On the other hand, a movement might be made with sudden
quickness such as starting to run on a signal.

2. *Force.* Force needs to be applied to set the body or one of its
segments in motion as well as to change its speed and/or direction. Thus,
force is concerned with how much strength is required for movement.
Swinging the arm in an axial movement requires less strength than
attempting to propel the body over the surface area with a standing
broad jump.

3. *Space.* In general, there are two factors concerned with space.
These are the amount of space required to perform a particular movement and the utilization of available space. With regard to the latter, it is
believed that young children during nonstructured self-initiated play
seem to reveal differences in the quantity of space they use, and that
these differences may be associated in important ways with other aspects
of the child's development. In fact, some studies tend to support the

concept that space utilization of the young child in active play is a relatively stable dimension of his patterned behavior.

4. *Flow.* All movements involve some degree of rhythm in their performance; thus, flow is concerned with sequence of movement involving rhythmic motion.

The above factors are included in all body movements in various degrees. The degree to which each is used effectively in combination will determine the extent to which the movement is performed with skill.

SKILL

It was mentioned previously that skill is concerned with the degree of proficiency with which a given body movement is performed. This is to say that skills are concerned with the scientific way to move the body and/or its segments in such a way as to expend a minimum of energy requirement, but achieve maximum results. Prominent neurophysiologists have suggested that skill is the putting together of simple natural movements, of which we have only about 200, in unusual or complex combinations to achieve a given objective. Performance of specific skills has been arrived at by scientific insight from such fields as anatomy and kinesiology which suggest to us how the body can move to achieve maximum efficiency.

Other things being equal, the degree of proficient performance of a skill by any individual is directly related to his innate capacity. That is, each individual is endowed with a certain amount of native ability. Through such factors as good teaching, motivation, and the like, attempts are made to help the child perform to the best of his or her particular ability, or to attain his or her highest *skill level.*

FACTORS INVOLVED IN
SKILL TEACHING AND LEARNING

Although a child is born with a certain potential capacity, teachers should not subscribe to the notion that skills are a part of the child's inheritance. Skills must be learned. In order that a child can participate satisfactorily with his or her peers, he or she must be given the opportunity to learn the skills under careful guidance of competent teachers.

The elementary school has long been considered the educational segment in an individual's life that provides the best opportunity for a solid educational foundation. The need for the development of basic skills in reading, writing, and arithmetic has seldom been challenged as an essential purpose of the elementary school. Why, then, should there be a neglect in some schools of such an important aspect of learning as that existing in the development of fundamental motor skills.

Perhaps the ideal time to learn motor skills is in childhood. The muscular pliability of the elementary school age child is such that there is a desirable setting for the acquisition of various kinds of motor skills. He or she is at a stage in life when there is a great deal of time for practice—a most important factor because a child needs practice in order to learn—and at this age level the child does not seem to become weary of repeating the same thing over and over again. In addition, the elementary school age child has a limited number of established skills to obstruct the learning of new skills. Skill learning therefore should be facilitated, provided competent teaching of motor skills is available. There should be little or no future problem of "unlearning" skills that the child might have had to learn incorrectly "on his own."

Experimental research on the influence of specific instruction on various kinds of motor skills is somewhat limited. More and more scientific evidence is being accumulated, however, which appears to indicate that children in the early elementary years are mature enough to benefit from instruction in such skills as throwing and jumping. Following are some suggested guidelines that teachers might take into account in the teaching of motor skills.

1. The teacher should become familiar with the skills involved in the activities in which a child will engage. This means that it will be necessary for the teacher to analyze each activity to determine the extent of the skill requirements.

2. In considering the teaching of motor skills, the teacher should recognize that skills include the following components: (a) preparing for the movement, (b) executing the movement, and (c) following through. For example, in throwing a ball the individual prepares for the movement by assuming the proper position to throw; he completes the actual throwing of the ball; and finally there is a follow-through action of the arm after the ball leaves the hand. All of these elements are essential to satisfactory performance of this particular skill.

3. The skill should be taught correctly from the beginning; otherwise

children may have to do a considerable amount of "unlearning" at a later stage of development.

4. When an error in skill performance is observed it should be corrected immediately. This can be done under the guidance of the teacher by evaluating the child's performance with him. Correction of errors in skill performance is essential; first, because continued repetition may formulate the faulty practice into a habit, and second, because the child will have less difficulty learning more complex skills if he has previously learned easier skills correctly. Teachers should recognize that while there are general patterns for the best performance of skills, individual differences must be considered. This implies that a child should be permitted to deviate from a standard if he is able to perform a skill satisfactorily in a manner peculiar to his individual abilities.

5. The greatest amount of time should be spent on skill learning that involves immediate application. In other words, the child should have use for the motor skills being taught so that he can properly apply them commensurate with his stage of development.

6. There is some indication that rhythmic accompaniment is important in the learning of skills. Although evidence is not definitive and clear-cut, various studies tend to support this contention. For example, some studies on the development of motor skills at the fifth-grade level have found that a conventional method of instruction supplemented by rhythmic accompaniment is superior to the conventional method without such accompaniment.

LOCOMOTOR SKILLS

In the previous discussion of locomotor movements it was indicated that the proficiency of these movements concerned the degree of skill involved in the execution of such movements. Thus, locomotor skills require a certain amount of strength and the development of the important sensory-motor mechanics that are concerned with balance. They also require various degrees of neuromotor coordination for proficient performance.

All of the locomotor skills should be learned by the elementary school child. The reason for this is that these skills comprise the basic requirements for proficiency of performance in the activities contained in the child's movements experiences. Teachers should have certain basic knowledge about the locomotor skills so that they will be alert to improve performance of these skills. The following generalized information is intended for this purpose.

Walking

Walking is the child's first experience with bipedal locomotion. He starts out to propel himself over the surface area with uneven full sole steps (flatfootedness). He is generally referred to as a "toddler," a term which is perhaps derived from the word "tottering." He appears to be tottering to keep in an upright position which is indicative of the problems he is having with balance and the force of gravity. At about four years of age, on the average, the child's pattern of walking approximates that of an adult.

Ordinarily, when the child is learning to walk, his only teachers are his family members. Because of this he is not likely to benefit from instruction on correct procedure. As a result, the very important aspect of foot position might be overlooked. Possibly because of this many children enter school walking in the "toeing out" position rather than pointing the toes straight ahead. Poor walking habits, if allowed to persist, can place undue amounts of strain on certain body parts which in turn can contribute to lack of proficiency in body movement.

Walking involves transferring the weight from one foot to the other. The walk is started with a push-off backward against the surface area with the ball and toes of the foot. After this initial movement the leg swings forward from the hip, the heel of the other foot is placed down, the outer half of the foot next, and then the next push-off is made with toes pointing straight ahead.

Running

At about 18 months of age the average child develops a movement that appears to be in between a walk and a run. This is to say that the walking pattern is accelerated but does not approximate running form. Usually, it is not before age five or six that the child's running form becomes like that used by an adult. As the child gets older he is able to increase his speed of running as well as to be able to run greater distances.

As in the case of walking, running involves transferring the weight from one foot to the other, but the rate of speed is increased. The ball of the foot touches the surface area first and the toes point straight ahead. The body is momentarily suspended in the air when there is no contact with the surface area. This differs from the walk in which contact with either foot is always maintained with the surface area. In the run there is more flexion at the knee which involves a higher leg lift. There is also a higher arm lift with flexion at the elbow reaching a point of about a right angle. In running there is more of a forward body lean than in walking and in both cases the head points straight ahead. In many instances the child who has not been taught to run correctly will violate certain mechanical principles by having a backward rather than forward lean, by carrying the arms too high, and by turning the head to the side rather than looking straight ahead.

Leaping

Leaping, like walking and running, is performed with an even rhythm, and is like a slow run with one essential difference. That is, the push-off is up and then forward, with the feeling of suspension "up and over." The landing should be on the ball of the foot with sufficient flexion at the knee to absorb the shock.

Jumping

In a sense, jumping is somewhat like walking and running as far as a movement pattern is concerned. However, jumping requires elevation of the body off the surface area and thus more strength is needed to apply force for this purpose. Usually, the child's first experience with a movement approximating jumping occurs when he steps from a higher to a lower level as in the case of going downstairs. Although there are many variations in jumping performance of children, generally speaking, they tend to improve their performance as they get older, with improvement tending to be more pronounced for boys than for girls.

Jumping is accomplished by pushing off with both feet and landing on both feet, or pushing off with one foot and landing on both feet. Since absorption of shock is important in the jump, the landing should be with flexed knees and on the balls of the feet.

Hopping

While hopping is the least difficult of the even rhythmic locomotor skills to describe, at the same time it is perhaps the most difficult to execute. Hopping involves taking off and landing on the same foot. Thus, hopping is a more complex aspect of the jump because the body is elevated from the surface area by the action of only one foot. Not only is greater strength needed for the hop, but also a more refined adjustment of balance is required because of the smaller base of support.

Even though hopping is not a specific skill that a child uses a great deal, one of the more important reasons why children should become proficient in this locomotor skill is that it can help them regain balance in any kind of activity where they have temporarily "lost their footing." When this occurs, the child can use the hop to keep his balance and remain in an upright position while getting the temporarily incapacitated foot into action.

Galloping

The skill of galloping is a combination of the basic patterns of walking and leaping and is performed with an uneven rhythm. Since an uneven rhythmic movement requires more neuromotor coordination, the ability to gallop is developed later than those locomotor movements requiring an even rhythm. The child is likely to learn to gallop before he learns to skip and about one-half of the children are able to perform a galloping movement by about the age of four. Between the ages of six and seven most children can perform this movement.

Galloping can be explained by pretending that one foot is injured. A step is taken with the lead foot, but the "injured" foot can bear very little weight and is brought up only behind the other one and not beyond it. A transfer of weight is made to the lead foot, and thus a fast limp is really a gallop.

One of the most important factors about learning how to gallop is that it helps children to be able to change direction in a forward or backward plane more easily. Backward galloping can be done by starting with the lead foot to the back. If a child is proficient in galloping, he will likely be more successful in activities that require a forward and/or backward movement for successful performance in that particular activity.

Skipping

Although skipping requires more coordination than galloping, some children will perform variations of the skip around four years of age. With proper instruction a majority of children should be able to accomplish this movement by age six.

Skipping can be taught from the walk. A strong push-off should be emphasized. The push-off should be such a forceful upward one that the foot leaves the surface area. In order to maintain balance a hop is taken. The sequence is step, push-off high, hop. The hop occurs on the same foot that was pushing off, and this is the skip. The two actions cause it to be an uneven rhythmic movement, with a strong or long action (step) and a short one (hop).

Sliding

Sliding is much the same as the gallop, but movement is in a sideward direction. One foot is drawn up to the lead foot; weight is shifted from the lead foot to the drawing foot and back again. As in the case with the other locomotor skills that are uneven in rhythm, sliding is not used frequently as a specific skill in most activities.

The important feature of gaining proficiency in the skill of sliding is that it helps the child to be able to change direction skillfully in a lateral plane. Many games involving guarding an opponent such as in basketball require skill in sliding for success in the game. When a child has developed the skill of sliding from side to side he does not have to cross his feet and thus can change direction laterally much more rapidly.

AXIAL SKILLS

It was mentioned previously that axial movements are nonlocomotor in nature. They can be performed with some parts of the body remaining in contact with the surface area or the body as a whole in gross movement. Included among the axial skills are swinging, bending, stretching, pulling, pushing, and the rotation movements of turning and twisting.

Each of these movements is required at one time or another in the performance of many activities. Proficiency of performance of the axial skills will improve performance in locomotor skills; for example, the importance of arm swinging in running. When children can perform the axial skills with grace and facility there is a minimum expenditure of energy and better performance results.

AUXILIARY SKILLS

There are certain skills that are not ordinarily classified as either locomotor or axial. However, they are most important in the successful performance of most activities. These skills are arbitrarily identified here as *auxiliary* skills. Among some of the more important of this type of skill are: starting, stopping, dodging, pivoting, falling, and landing.

Starting

In games that require responding to a stimulus such as running to a goal on the word "go" a quick start is an important contribution to success. How well a child will be able to "start" depends upon his reaction time and speed of movement. Reaction time is the amount of time that it takes from the time a signal is given until the initial movement. Speed of movement is concerned with how fast a person completes the initial movement. Although the factors concerned with starting are innate, they improve with age and they can be improved with practice. When a teacher observes children as being "slow starters," additional help should be given to improve this skill.

Stopping

The skill of stopping is very important because all locomotor movements culminate with this skill. Numerous activities require quick stopping for successful performance.

The two ways of stopping are the *stride* stop and the *skip* stop. The stride stop involves stopping in running stride. There is flexion at the knees and there is a slight backward lean to maintain balance. This method of stopping can be used when the performer is moving at slow speed. The skip stop should be used when there is fast movement and the performer needs to come to a quick stop. This is accomplished with a hop on either foot with the other foot making contact with the surface area almost simultaneously. Because of the latter movement, this method of stopping is sometimes called the *jump* stop because it appears that the performer is landing on both feet.

Starting and stopping can be practiced in a game situation with the game of "Start and Stop." In this game the children are in a straight line with the teacher at a goal line some distance away. The teacher calls "Start," and on this signal all children run forward. The teacher calls "Stop," and anyone moving after the signal must return to the starting line. This procedure is continued until one or more children have reached the goal line. The teacher should be alert to detect starting and stopping form.

Dodging

Dodging involves changing body direction while running. The knees are bent, and the weight is transferred in the dodging direction. This movement is sometimes referred to as "veering" or "weaving." After a dodge is made, the performer can continue in the different direction with a push-off from the surface area with the foot to which the weight was previously transferred.

The importance of skill in dodging is seen in game activities where getting away from an opponent (tag games) or an object (dodge ball) is concerned.

Pivoting

Whereas dodging is used to change direction during body movement, pivoting is employed to change direction while the body is stationary. One foot is kept in contact with the surface area, while the other foot is used to push off. A turn is made in the desired direction with the weight on the foot that has maintained contact with the surface area. The angle of the pivot (turn) is determined by the need in a particular situation. This angle is seldom over 180 degrees as might be the case in pivoting away from an opponent in basketball.

Theoretically, the pivot is executed on only one foot; however, a *reverse turn* is sometimes referred to as a "two-foot" pivot. In this case a complete turn to the opposite direction is made with both feet on the surface area. With one foot ahead of the other, the heels are raised and a turn is made with the weight equally distributed on both feet.

Landing

Landing is concerned with the body coming to the surface area from a height or distance. Absorption when landing is accomplished by bending the knees. The weight is on the balls of the feet and there is flexion at the ankle and knee joints. After landing, the performer comes to an upright position with the arms in a sideward position so as to keep the body in balance.

Falling

In those activities that require keeping in an upright position, emphasis, of course, should be on maintaining this position. Nevertheless, there are occasions when a performer loses balance and falls to the surface area. Whenever possible, a fall should be taken in such a way that injury is least likely to occur. One way to accomplish this is to attempt to "break the fall" with the hands. Relaxation and flexion at the joints that put the performer in a "bunched" position are helpful in avoiding injury when falling to the surface area.

SKILLS OF PROPULSION AND RETRIEVAL

Skills which involve propelling and retrieving objects, in most cases a ball,[1] are used in many types of game activities. It will be the purpose of the ensuing sections of this chapter to provide the reader with knowledge which is important to an understanding of such propelling and retrieving skills as throwing, striking, kicking, and catching.

Throwing

The skill of throwing involves the release of a ball with one or both hands. In general, there are three factors concerned with success in throwing. These are the accuracy or direction of the throw, the distance which a ball must be thrown, and the amount of force needed to propel the ball.

Any release of an object from the hand or hands could be considered as an act of throwing. Thought of in these terms the average infant of six

---

[1]Hereafter in this discussion the object propelled or retrieved will be referred to as "the ball."

months of age is able to perform a reasonable facsimile of throwing from a sitting position. It has been estimated that by four years of age, about 20 percent of the children show at least a degree of proficiency in throwing. This ability tends to increase rapidly, and between the ages of five and six, over three-fourths of the children have attained a reasonable degree of proficiency as previously defined here.

Sex differences in the early throwing behavior of children tend to favor boys. At all age levels boys are generally superior to girls in throwing for distance. There is not such a pronounced sex difference in throwing for accuracy, although the performance of boys in this aspect tends to exceed that of girls.

There are three generally accepted throwing *patterns.* These are the (1) underarm pattern; (2) sidearm pattern; and (3) overarm pattern. It should be noted that although the ball released by one or both hands, the term "arm" is used in connection with the various patterns. The reason for this is that the patterns involve a "swing" of the arm.

Underarm Throwing Pattern

The child ordinarily begins the underarm throwing pattern by releasing the ball from both hands. However, he is soon able to release with one hand, especially when the ball is small enough for him to grip.

At the starting position the thrower stands facing in the direction of the throw. The feet should be in a parallel position and slightly apart. The right arm[2] is in a position nearly perpendicular to the surface area. To start the throw, the right arm is brought back (back swing) to a position where it is about parallel with the surface area. Simultaneously, there is slight rotation of the body to the right with most of the weight transferred to the right foot. As the arm comes forward (front swing) a step is taken with the left foot. (Stepping out with the opposite foot of the swinging arm is known as the *principle of opposition*). The ball is released on the front swing when the arm is about parallel with the surface area. During the process of the arm swing, the arm is straight, prescribing a semicircle with no flexion at the elbow. The right foot is carried forward as a part of the follow-through after the release.

---

[2]All of the descriptions involving the skills of propulsion and retrieval are for a right-handed child. In the case of the left-handed child, just the opposite should apply.

Sidearm Throwing Pattern

Aside from the direction the thrower faces and the plane of the arm swing, the mechanical principles applied in the sidearm throwing pattern are essentially the same as the underarm throwing pattern.

The thrower faces at a right angle to the direction of the throw, whereas in the underarm throwing pattern he faces in the direction of the throw. The arm is brought to the backswing in a horizontal plane, or a position parallel to the surface area. Body rotation and weight shift is the same as in the underarm pattern. The arm remains straight and a semicircle is prescribed from the backswing to the release of the ball on the front swing.

The sidearm throwing pattern will ordinarily be used to propel a ball that is too large to grip with one hand. Thus, on the backswing the opposite hand helps to control the ball until there is sufficient momentum during the swing. Greater distance can be obtained with the sidearm throwing pattern with a ball too large to grip, but accuracy is more difficult to achieve.

Overarm Throwing Pattern

Again the basic body mechanics of the overarm throwing pattern are essentially the same as the two previous patterns. The thrower faces in the same direction as for the sidearm throwing pattern; that is, at a right angle to the direction of the throw. An essential difference in the overarm throwing pattern is in the position of the arm. Whereas in the two previous patterns the arm was kept straight, in the overarm throwing pattern there is flexion at the elbow. Thus, on the backswing the arm is brought back with the elbow bent and with the arm at a right angle away from the body. The arm is then brought forward and the ball is released with a "whiplike" motion at about the height of the shoulder. Foot and arm follow-through is the same as with the underarm and sidearm throwing patterns. This pattern is used for throwing a ball that can be gripped with the fingers where distance as well as accuracy is important.

Striking

Striking involves propelling a ball with a part of the body, ordinarily the hand, as in handball, or with an implement such as a bat in softball. The object to be struck can be stationary (as batting a ball from a batting tee) or moving (as batting a pitched ball in softball).

Some motor development specialists have identified a reasonable facsimile of striking in infancy associated with angry children throwing "nothing" at each other or an adult.

There is some evidence to support the notion that as early as the age of three, verbal direction to the child will educe a sidearm striking pattern with a plastic paddle, when a tennis ball is suspended in a stationary position at about waist high. In addition, it has been found that at age three the child will have a degree of success with the sidearm throwing pattern in striking a light ball when tossed slowly to him.

As far as principles of body mechanics are concerned, striking patterns are essentially the same as the three previously mentioned throwing patterns; that is, underarm, sidearm, and overarm. The same movements are applied, but in order to propel an object by striking, greater speed is needed with the striking movement.

Kicking

Kicking involves propelling a ball with either foot. As early as age two the average child is able to maintain his balance on one foot and propel a stationary ball with the other foot. At this early stage the child is likely to have limited action of the kicking foot with little or no follow-through. With advancing age, better balance is maintained and with greater increments of strength, by age six the child can develop a full leg backswing and a body lean into the kick with a stationary ball.

In kicking, contact with the ball is made with the (1) inside of the foot, (2) outside of the foot, or, (3) with the instep of the foot. With the exception of these positions of the foot the mechanical principles of kicking are essentially the same. The kicking leg is swung back with flexion at the knee. The leg swings forward with the foot making contact with the ball. As in the case of the skill of striking, contact with the ball in kicking can be made when the ball is either stationary or moving.

There is not complete agreement in terms of progression in the skill of kicking. The following sequence is recommended by the present authors:

1. *Stationary.* The ball and the kicker remain stationary. That is, the kicker stands beside the ball and kicks it. The kicker is concerned only with the leg movement, and it is more likely that he will keep his head down with his eyes on the ball at the point of contact.

2. *Stationary and run.* This means that the ball is in a stationary position and that the kicker takes a short run up to the ball before kicking

it. This is more difficult as the kicker must time and coordinate his run to make proper contact with the ball.

3. *Kick from hands.* This is referred to as "punting" as in football, soccer, and speedball. The ball is dropped from the hands of the kicker and he takes one or two steps and kicks the ball as it drops. He is kicking a moving ball but he has control over the movement of the ball before kicking it.

4. *Kicking from a pitcher.* This means that another person pitches or rolls the ball to the kicker as in the game of Kickball. This is perhaps the most difficult kick because the kicker must kick a moving ball that is under the control of another person.

Catching

Catching with the hands is the most frequently used retrieving skill although, a ball can be retrieved with the feet as in "trapping" the ball in soccer.

One of the child's first experiences with catching occurs at an early age in life when he sits with his legs in a spread position and another person rolls a ball to him. By four years of age about one-third of the children can retrieve a ball in aerial flight thrown from a short distance. Slightly over half of them can perform this feat by age five, and about two-thirds of them can accomplish this by age six.

Generally speaking, it has been observed that children achieve the same skill level sooner in catching with a larger ball than they do with a smaller ball. It has been found that ball size does not generally differentiate between success and failure in catching. Size of ball, however, seems to make a difference in the type of catch utilized by children. The arms and body may be used more frequently with a larger ball, resulting in a "basket catch." There appears to be more hand closure success with the smaller ball.

In recent years studies have been conducted in an attempt to determine effects of velocity, projective angle, and time of ball in flight. Studies of second-fourth-and sixth grade boys and girls show that catching performance improves with grade level; that boys may be superior to girls in catching performance; that younger, lesser skilled children show poorer performance as ball velocity increases; and that changes in vertical angle of projection has little effect on catching performance. It is further indicated that variation in time of ball flight has no significant effect on catching performance.

There are certain basic mechanical principles that should be taken into account in the skill of catching. It is of utmost importance that the catcher position himself as nearly "in line" with the ball as possible. In this position he will be better able to receive the ball near the center of gravity of the body. Another important factor is hand position. A ball will approach the catcher (1) at the waist, (2) above the waist, or (3) below the waist. When the ball approaches at about waist level, the palms should be facing each other with fingers pointing straight ahead. The "heels" of the hands should be close together depending upon the size of the ball. That is, closer together for a small ball and farther apart for a large ball. When the ball approaches above the waist the palms face the ball and fingers point upward with the thumbs as close together as necessary. When the ball approaches below the waist the palms still face the ball but the fingers point downward with the little fingers as close together as seems necessary, depending again upon the size of the ball. When the ball reaches the hands it is brought in toward the body. That is, the catcher "gives" with the catch in order to control the ball and absorb the shock. The position of the feet will likely depend upon the speed with which the ball approaches. Ordinarily, one foot should be in advance of the other in a stride position, with the distance determined by the speed of the approaching ball.

Chapter 4

SOCIAL DEVELOPMENT

Social development is so comprehensive that it has been described in a number of ways as follows: (1) the pattern of change through the years exhibited by the individual as a result of his interaction with such forces as people, social institutions, social customs, and social organizations; (2) the entire series of progressive changes from birth to death in social behavior, feelings, attitudes, values, etc. that are normal for the individuals of a species; (3) the state of any moment of an individual's social or socially significant reaction, evaluated in accordance with what is regarded as normal for that culture; (4) the growth of the culture of the group in the direction of the more complete satisfaction of the needs of its members.[1]

SOCIAL NEEDS OF CHILDREN

The importance of social needs is brought more clearly into focus when we consider that most of what human beings do they do together. Social maturity, and thus social fitness—so important to social development—might well be expressed in terms of the fulfillment of certain needs. In other words, if certain social needs are being met, the child should be in a better position to realize social fitness. Among other needs, we must give consideration to (1) the need for *affection* which involves acceptance and approval by persons; (2) the need for *belonging* which involves acceptance and approval of the group; and (3) the need for *mutuality* which involves cooperation, mutual helpfulness, and group loyalty.

When it comes to evaluating social outcomes, we do not have the same kind of objective instruments that are available in computing accurately the physical attributes of children. In some cases (and primarily for diagnostic purposes) in dealing with children some school systems have successfully used some of the acceptable *sociometric* techniques. However, at best the social aspect is difficult to appraise objectively because of its

---

[1]Good, Carter V., *Dictionary of Education*, New York, McGraw-Hill Book Company, 1959, p. 168.

somewhat vague nature. (These techniques will be discussed later in the chapter.)

In addition to the general social needs previously mentioned, specific needs are reflected in the developmental traits and characteristics of growing children. Many such characteristics are identified in the following lists at the different age levels.

Five-Year-Old Children

1. Interested in neighborhood games that involve any number of children.
2. Plays various games to test his skill.
3. Enjoys other children and likes to be with them.
4. Interests are largely self-centered.
5. Seems to get along best in small groups.
6. Shows an interest in home activities.
7. Imitates when he plays.
8. Gets along well in taking turns.
9. Respects the belongings of other people.

Six-Year-Old Children

1. Self-centered and has need for praise.
2. Likes to be first.
3. Indifferent to sex distinction.
4. Enjoys group play when groups tend to be small.
5. Likes parties but behavior may not always be decorous.
6. The majority enjoy school association and have a desire to learn.
7. Interests in conduct of his friends.
8. Boys like to fight and wrestle with peers to prove masculinity.
9. Shows an interest in group approval.

Seven-Year-Old Children

1. Wants recognition for his individual achievements.
2. Sex differences are not of great importance.
3. Not always a good loser.
4. Conversation often centers around family.

5. Learning to stand up for his own rights.
6. Interested in friends and is not influenced by their social or economic status.
7. May have nervous habits such as nail biting, tongue sucking, scratching, or pulling at ear.
8. Attaining orientation in time.
9. Gets greater enjoyment from group play.
10. Shows greater signs of cooperative efforts.

Eight-Year-Old Children

1. Girls are careful of their clothes, but boys are not.
2. Leaves many things uncompleted.
3. Has special friends.
4. Has longer periods of peaceful play.
5. Does not like playing alone.
6. Enjoys dramatizing.
7. Starts collections.
8. Enjoys school and dislikes staying home.
9. Likes variety.
10. Recognition of property rights is well established.
11. Responds well to group activity.
12. Interest will focus on friends of own sex.
13. Beginning of the desire to become a member of the club.

Nine-Year-Old Children

1. Wants to be like others, talk like others, and look like them.
2. Girls are becoming more interested in their clothes.
3. Is generally a conformist and may be afraid of that which is different.
4. Able to be on his own.
5. Able to be fairly responsible and dependable.
6. Some firm and loyal friendships may develop.
7. Increasing development of qualities of leadership and followership.
8. Increasing interest in activities involving challenges and adventure.
9. Increasing participation in varied and organized group activities.

Ten-Year-Old Children

1. Begins to recognize the fallibility of adults.
2. Moving more into a peer-centered society.
3. Both boys and girls are amazingly self-dependent.
4. Self-reliance has grown and at the same time intensified group feelings are required.
5. Divergence between the two sexes is widening.
6. Great team loyalties are developing.
7. Beginning to identify with one's social contemporaries of the same sex.
8. Relatively easy to appeal to his reason.
9. On the whole, he has a fairly critical sense of justice.
10. Boys show their friendship with other boys by wrestling and jostling with each other, while girls walk around with arms around each other as friends.
11. Interest in people, in the community, and in affairs of the world is keen.
12. Interested in social problems in an elementary way and likes to take part in discussions.

Eleven-Year-Old Children

1. Internal guiding standards have been set up, and although guided by what is done by other children, he will modify his behavior in line with those standards already set up.
2. Does a number of socially acceptable things, not because they are right *or* wrong.
3. Although obsessed by standards of peers, he is anxious for social approval of adults.
4. Need for social companionship of children their own age.
5. Liking for organized games becoming more prominent.
6. Girls are likely to be self-conscious in the presence of boys and are usually much more mature than boys.
7. Team spirit is very strong.
8. Boys' and girls' interests are not always the same, and there may be some antagonism between the sexes.
9. Often engages in silly behavior, such as giggling and clowning.
10. Girls are more interested in social appearance than are boys.

Twelve-Year-Old Children

1. Increasing identification of self with other children of his own sex.
2. Increasing recognition of fallibility of adults.
3. May see himself as a child and adults as adults.
4. Getting ready to make the difficult transition to adolescence.
5. Pressure is being placed on individual at this level to begin to assume adult responsibilities.

It should be obvious that the above social characteristics of different age children should be taken into account if we are to meet with any degree of success in our efforts in the direction of social development.

GUIDELINES FOR SOCIAL DEVELOPMENT

Guidelines for social development are set forth here in the same manner that guidelines for physical development were proposed in Chapter 2. That is, these guidelines take the form of valid *concepts of social development.* When we have some basis for the social behavior of children as they grow and develop we are then in a better position to select and conduct experiences that are likely to be compatible with social development. The following list of concepts of social development are submitted with this general idea in mind.

1. *Interpersonal relationships are based on social needs.* All children should be given an equal opportunity in participation. Moreover, the teacher should impress upon children their importance to the group. This can be done in connection with most group efforts, which is so essential to successful participation.

2. *A child can develop his or her self-concept through undertaking roles.* A child is more likely to be aware of his or her particular abilities if given the opportunity to play different roles in school situations. Rotation of such responsibilities as group leaders and committee assignments tends to provide opportunity for self-expression of children through role playing.

3. *There are various degrees of interaction between individuals and groups.* School experiences should provide for settings for the child to develop interpersonal interaction. The teacher has the opportunity to observe children in various situations. Consequently, the teacher is in a good position to guide integrative experiences by helping children to

see the importance of satisfactory interrelationships in certain group situations.

4. *Choosing and being chosen—an expression of a basic need—is a foundation of interpersonal relationships.* As often as possible, children should be given the opportunity for choosing teammates, partners, and the like. However, great caution should be taken by the teacher to see that this is carried out in an equitable way. The teacher should devise ways of choice so that certain children are not always selected last or left out entirely.

5. *Language is a basic means and essential accompaniment of socialization.* Children can be taught the language of the body through using the names of its parts. This is an important dimension in the development of body awareness. School experiences should be such that there is opportunity for oral expression among and between children. For example, in the evaluation phase of a lesson, children have a fine opportunity for meaningful oral expression if the evaluation is skillfully guided by the teacher.

6. *Learning to play roles is a process of social development.* A child should be given the opportunity to play as many roles as possible in his or her school experiences. This could being involved in the organization of class activities.

7. *Integrative interaction tends to promote social development.* Spontaneity can be considered as one of the desired outcomes of integrative experiences, which means the opportunity for actions and feelings expressed by the child as he or she really is.

8. *Resistance to domination is an active attempt to maintain one's integrity.* The teacher might well consider child resistance as a possible indicator of teacher domination. If this occurs, the teacher might look into his or her actions, which may be dominating the teaching-learning situation. Child resistance should be interpreted as a sign of a healthful personality, and a wise teacher will likely be able to direct the energy into constructive channels to promote social development.

9. *Interpersonal interaction between children is a basis for choice.* If children are left out by other children, this symptom should be studied with care to see if this is an indication of poor interpersonal relationships with other children. Very interesting aspects of interpersonal relationships can be observed by the wise teacher. Children may realize the value of a child to a specific activity and accept such a child accordingly. On the other hand, they may be likely to accept their friends regardless of their ability.

10. *A child, in and as a result of belonging to a group develops differently than he or she can as an individual alone.* Many school activities provide for an outstanding opportunity for children to engage actively in a variety of group experiences. Merely being a member of a group can be a most rewarding experience for a child. If properly conducted, many group activities should provide an optimal situation for desirable social development.

SOME POSSIBILITIES FOR SOCIAL DEVELOPMENT THROUGH CERTAIN SCHOOL EXPERIENCES

There are various school situations through which children may gain a better understanding of the importance of cooperation. For example, the many games that children engage in in the school physical education program depend upon the cooperation of group members in achieving a common goal. Dancing as a part of the music and/or physical education programs is an activity that requires persons to perform together in a synchronization of rhythmic patterns. It has been demonstrated on numerous occasions that children can gain insight into the way of life of our own people and people of other lands by learning dances engaged in by these people. Early American country dances and nationality dances provide children with an opportunity to see the significance between the activities and the cultural and physical aspects that bear upon them.

During recess periods leadership and followership may be found in games such as *Follow the Leader,* with one child selected to be the leader and others following and attempting to do the same things. In the same context, group consciousness and friendliness within a group can be developed in certain activities. For example, some teachers feel that games played from a circle formation have a positive effect in that they tend to provide a spirit of unity among the participants; that is, each player can see and become aware of the performance of other players in the group. It is interesting to note that holding hands in a circle game has important connotations for social interaction through *tactile communication.* The possibilities of this suggest that better human relations can be obtained through intrinsic tactile communication in the utilization of activities requiring *touch.* In fact, some studies substantiate the idea that such tactile communication provides a basis for the attraction that is necessary for black and white children to form positive relationships.

More specifically, recorded incidents of tactile interaction between black and white children appear to be equivalent to the recorded incidents of tactile interaction between black children and black children and those between white and white children.

In spite of such findings, circle games have been much maligned on the basis that there is too much inactivity of children just standing in a circle. It is doubtful if such criticism is entirely justified, because the skillful teacher can conduct this type of activity in such a way that there will be equal opportunity for participation.

The natural opportunities for wholesome group experiences in games provide a means for the development of ability to get along with various kinds of people. One teacher, confronted with the problem of getting a fourth-grade class to be more congenial employed the game called *Hook On*. In one version of this game, one player is selected to be *IT* and another is selected to be the chaser. These two take positions at opposite ends of the activity area. The other players form couples by linking arms with a partner, and the couples take places anywhere in the playing area. At a signal, the chaser attempts to tag *IT*, who dodges in and out between the couples. In order to avoid being tagged, *IT* can "hook on" to a free arm of one of the couples. At this time, the other person of that couple becomes *IT*, and the game proceeds in this manner. The teacher found that this particular activity helped to eliminate certain cliques that were being formed in the class. She noticed that children did not always hook on to their friends, since out of necessity they needed to hook on to any available couple to avoid being tagged.

Issues that might come up as a result of certain misunderstandings in some school situations give rise to the exercise of wholesome social controls. The relationships of these controls in school experiences to those in community living might possibly be understood in various degrees by children at the different age levels. In these situations, outstanding settings can be provided for the development of problem-solving techniques in which children are placed to make value judgments.

IMPLICATIONS OF RESEARCH IN SOCIAL BEHAVIOR OF CHILDREN

There has been an appreciable amount of research regarding social development of children. This being the case, we should perhaps consider some of this research so that we can draw some implications for certain school experiences. This is to say that in utilizing such findings, we will be better able to conduct school experiences that will be more likely to result in positive social development. A report by the National Institute of Education has provided some information that should be useful for this purpose.[2]

The purpose of the report was to provide preschool and early elementary school teachers with a summary of current *psychological* research concerned with the social development of young children. In submitting the report, the authors noted that caution should prevail with reference to basic research and practical implications. In this regard, the following suggestions are submitted.

1. What seems "true" at one point in time often becomes "false" when new information becomes available or when new theories change the interpretation of old findings.
2. Substantial problems arise in any attempt to formulate practical suggestions for professionals in one discipline based on research findings from another discipline.
3. Throughout the report, recommendations for teachers have been derived from logical extensions of experimental findings and classroom adaptations of experimental procedures.
4. Some of the proposed procedures may prove unworkable in the classroom, even though they may make sense from a psychological perspective.
5. When evaluating potential applications of psychological findings it is important to remember that psychological research is usually designed to derive probability statements about the behavior of groups of people.
6. Individual teachers may work better with a procedure that is, on the average, less effective.

The following list of generalizations have been derived from the findings. In considering these generalizations the above cautions should be kept in mind. Moreover, each individual teacher will no doubt be able to draw his or her own implications and make practical applications that apply to particular situations.

---

[2]Roedell, W., Slaby, R. G., and Robinson, H. B., Social development in young children, a report for teachers, Washington, DC, National Institute of Education, U.S. Department of Health, Education and Welfare, January 1976.

1. *Reasoning with an emphasis on consequences for other people is associated with the development of a humanistic concern for others.* Teachers might consider encouragement of social behavior in school experiences by discussing the implications of children's and teachers' actions for the feelings of others; poor performers should be encouraged rather than ridiculed.

2. *Children tend to show empathy toward individuals similar to themselves.* In school experiences it is important to emphasize the likenesses of people; while all children may differ in one or more characteristics, they still are more alike than they are different.

3. *Children may learn techniques for positive social interaction by observing children who are behaving cooperatively.* In certain activities, cooperation of each individual is very important to the success of the group; the teacher can suggest ways children can cooperate and reinforce children when these suggestions are followed.

4. *The more frequently children voluntarily practice social skills, the more likely they are to use these skills in less structured situations.* In some school situations children can be assigned certain responsibilities that require the practice of social skills.

5. *Children are likely to use behaviors for which they have been reinforced.* The teacher can focus his or her attention on children who are cooperating, sharing, and helping the teacher and other children in the various school situations.

6. *Children are likely to imitate behaviors for which they see other children being reinforced.* The teacher can compliment those children who are saying cooperative, helpful things to each other. At the same time, the teacher should consider simultaneously ignoring negative social interactions of children.

7. *Children are likely to help and share when they have seen someone else do it, particularly if they know and like the model.* The teacher can take the lead by providing examples of sharing, helping, and cooperating.

8. *Ignored behavior may increase at first, but eventually it is likely to decrease if the child does not receive reinforcement from other sources.* The teacher may wish to pointedly ignore misbehavior whenever possible by turning away from the misbehaving child and attending to a child who is behaving appropriately. Obviously, all misbehavior cannot be ignored because in some instances such misbehavior might be concerned with safety factors. Thus, it is sometimes appropriate for the teacher to act expediently.

9. *Consistent, immediate punishment may tend to discourage the behavior it follows.* When it is necessary, the teacher might consider choosing mild punishment related to the activity, which can follow misbehavior immediately. For example, if a child is misusing a piece of material, it can be removed, at least temporarily.

10. *Reasoning can increase children's awareness of the needs of others, and it (reasoning) is a form of attention that should be limited to occasions when children are behaving appropriately.* In many teaching-learning situations there is a need for certain rules and regulations. It might be well to discuss the reasoning behind rules when children are following the rules and *not* when the rules are disobeyed. However, this does not necessarily preclude a negative approach if a given situation warrants it.

In closing this discussion, it should be reiterated that each individual reader will no doubt be able to draw his or her own implications and make practical applications that apply to particular school situations.

EVALUATING CONTRIBUTIONS OF SCHOOL EXPERIENCES TO SOCIAL DEVELOPMENT

In the past, most of what has been done in evaluating social growth in school has been of a subjective nature. The process of "observation" has been considered satisfactory, because it has been felt that for the most part we can merely watch children to see the kinds of relationships that exist between them.

Some educators have approached this problem from a more scientific standpoint and have used certain *sociometric techniques* with varying degrees of success. Included among such techniques are (1) sociograms, (2) sociographs, and (3) social distance scales.

Sociograms

In this technique, a child is usually asked to name in order of preference those persons liked best in a group. A child may be asked to name those he or she would like to be with or play with most. After the choices are made, the results are plotted on a sociogram.

If two children choose each other, they are known as "mutual choices of pairs." Those not selected by anyone in the group and who do not choose anyone are called "isolates." "Islands" is the name given to pairs or small groups of mutual choices not selected by any in the large group. While the sociogram is a worthwhile device for identifying certain aspects of interpersonal relationships, it is a time-consuming procedure and for this reason is not one of the more popular methods used by teachers.

Sociographs

The sociograph is a more expedient and practical way of tabulating and interpreting data. Instead of plotting as in a sociogram, choices are recorded in tabular form opposite the names of children. This readily shows the number of rejections, mutual choices, choices received, and choices given.

Social Distance Scales

This sociometric technique has been used in research in social psychology for well over fifty years. In this procedure, each member of a group is asked to check the other members according to certain degrees of social intimacy such as:

1. Would like to have him as one of my best friends.
2. Would like to have him in my group, but not as a close friend.
3. Would like to be with him once in a while, but not often or for very long.
4. Do not mind his being in the group, but I do not want anything to do with him.
5. Wish he were not in the group.

This procedure can be used as a classroom social distance scale to attempt to determine the general social tone of a particular class. Classroom social distance scores on each individual child can be obtained by arbitrarily weighting the items listed above. For example, if a child was checked two time for item number one ($2 \times 1 = 2$); six times for item two ($6 \times 2 = 12$); eight times for item three ($8 \times 3 = 24$); three times for item four ($3 \times 4 = 12$); and one time for item five ($1 \times 5 = 5$) the total score would be 55. (The lower the score the greater the acceptance by the group and the less the social distance.)

These data can used to determine, with some degree of objectivity, the extent to which certain school experiences have contributed to social relationships, that is, a teacher can compare scores before and after a group of children have been involved in a particular experience.

Over a period of years, we have used all of the above sociometric techniques with varying degrees of success. In some instances, the results have provided guidance in efforts to obtain a better understanding of social relationships and thus contribute to social development. It is recognized that all teachers are aware of those obvious factors concerned with group social structure. However, the many aspects of interpersonal relationships that are not so obvious can be difficult to discern. It is the purpose of sociometric techniques to assist in the emergence of these relationships.

Chapter 5

EMOTIONAL DEVELOPMENT

At one time or another, all of us (children and teachers alike) demon-strate emotional as well as ordinary behavior. Teachers and other adults should not necessarily think in terms of always suppressing the emotions of children. On the contrary, the goal should be to help chil-dren express their emotions as harmlessly as possible when they do occur so that emotional stability will be maintained. If this can be accomplished, problems resulting from harmful emotional behavior can at least be reduced, if not eliminated entirely.

As mentioned in Chapter 1, emotional patterns can be arbitrarily placed into the two broad categories of *pleasant* emotions and *unpleasant* emotions. Pleasant emotional patterns can include such feelings as joy, affection, happiness, and love, while unpleasant emotional patterns can include anger, sorrow, jealousy, fear, and worry — an imaginary form of fear.

The pleasantness or unpleasantness of an emotion seems to be deter-mined by its strength or intensity, by the nature of the situation arousing it, and by the way the child perceives or interprets the situation.

The ancient Greeks identified emotions with certain organs of the body, For example, in general sorrow was expressed from the heart (a broken heart), jealousy was associated with the liver, hate from the gallbladder, and anger with the spleen. In this regard, we sometimes hear the expression "venting the spleen" on someone. This historical reference is made, because in modern times we have taken into account certain conduits between emotions and the body. These are by way of the nervous system and the endocrine system. That part of the nervous system principally concerned with the emotions is the *autonomic* nervous system which controls functions such as the heart beat, blood pressure, and digestion. When there is a stimulus of any of the emotional patterns, these two systems activate. By way of illustration, if the emotional pat-tern of fear is stimulated the heartbeat accelerates, breathing is more rapid, and the blood pressure is likely to rise. Energy fuel is discharged into the blood from storage in the liver, which causes the blood sugar level to rise. These, along with other bodily functions, serve to prepare a person for coping with the condition caused by the fear.

Dealing with childhood emotions implies that sympathetic guidance should be provided in meeting anxieties, joys, and sorrows, and that help should be given in developing aspirations and security. In order to attempt to reach this objective, we might well consider emotions from a standpoint of the growing child maturing emotionally.

For purposes of this discussion *maturity* is considered as concerned with a state of *readiness* on the part of the organism. The term is most frequently used in connection with age relationships. For example, it may be said that "Johnny is mature for six years of age." Simply stated, *emotional maturity* is the process of acting one's age.

Generally speaking, emotional maturity will be achieved through a gradual accumulation of mild and pleasant emotions. Emotional *immaturity* indicates that unpleasant emotions have accumulated too rapidly for the child to absorb. One of the important factors in this regard is the process of *adjustment*, which can be described as the process of finding and adopting modes of behavior suitable to the environment or to changes in the environment.

The child's world involves a sequence of experiences that are characterized by the necessity for him to adjust. Consequently, it may be said that "normal" behavior is the result of successful adjustment and that abnormal behavior results from unsuccessful adjustment. The degree of adjustment that the child achieves depends upon how adequately he is able to satisfy his basic needs and to fulfill his desires within the framework of his environment and the pattern of ways dictated by society.

When the child's needs (basic demands) are not met and his or her desires (wants and wishes) are not satisfied, *frustration* or *conflict* result. Frustration occurs when a need is not met, and conflict results when: (1) choices must be made between nearly equally attractive alternatives, or (2) when basic emotional forces oppose one another. In an emotionally healthy child the degree of frustration is ordinarily in proportion to the intensity of the need or desire. That is, he or she will objectively observe and evaluate the situation to ascertain whether a solution is possible and, if so, what solution would best enable him or her to achieve the fulfillment of needs or desires.

In order to counteract some of the above problems and to be able to pursue a sensible course in helping children become more emotionally mature, there are certain factors concerned with emotional development of children that need to be taken into account. Some of these factors are the subject of the ensuing discussion.

FACTORS CONCERNING EMOTIONAL DEVELOPMENT

Some of the factors concerned with emotional development of children that need to be considered are: (1) characteristics of childhood emotionality, (2) emotional arousals and reactions, and (3) factors that influence emotionality.

Characteristics of Childhood Emotionality

Ordinarily the Emotions of Children Are Not Long Lasting

A child's emotions may last for a few minutes and then terminate rather abruptly. The child gets it "out of his system" so to speak, by expressing it outwardly. In contrast, some adult emotions may be long and drawn out. As children get older, expressing the emotions by overt action is encumbered by certain social restraints. This is to say that what might be socially acceptable at one age level is not necessarily so at another. This may be a reason for some children developing *moods*, which in a sense are states of emotion drawn out over a period of time and expressed slowly. Typical moods of childhood may be "sulking" due to restraint of anger, being "jumpy" from repressed fear, and becoming "humorous" from controlled joy or happiness.

The Emotions of Children Are Likely To Be Intense

This might be confusing to some adults who do not understand child behavior. That is, they may not be able to see why a child would react rather violently to a situation that to them might appear insignificant.

The Emotions of Children Are Subject to Rapid Change

A child is capable of shifting rapidly from laughing to crying or from anger to joy. Although the reason for this is not definitely known, it might be that there is not as much depth of feeling among children as there is among adults. In addition, it could be due to lack of experience that children have had, as well as their state of intellectual development. We do know that young children have a short attention span that could cause them to change rapidly from one kind of emotion to another.

The Emotions of Children Can Appear With a High Degree of Frequency

As children get older they manage to develop the ability to adjust to situations that previously would have caused an emotional reaction. This is probably due to the child's acquiring more experience with various kinds of emotional situations. Perhaps a child learns through experience what is socially acceptable and what is socially unacceptable. This is particularly true if the child is reprimanded in some way following a violent emotional reaction. For this reason, the child may try to confront situations in ways that do not involve an emotional response.

Children Differ in Their Emotional Responses

One child confronted with a situation that instills fear may run away from the immediate environment. Another may hide behind his mother. Still another might just stand there and cry. Different reactions of children to emotional situations are probably due to a host of factors. Included among these may be past experiences with a certain kind of emotional situation, willingness of parents and other adults to help children become independent, and family relationships in general.

Strength of Children's Emotions Are Subject to Change

At some age levels certain kinds of emotions may be weak and later become stronger. Conversely, with some children emotions that were strong may tend to decline. For example, small children may be timid among strangers, but later, when they see there is little to fear, the timidity is likely to wane.

Emotional Arousals and Reactions

If we are to understand the emotions of children, we need to take into account those factors of emotional arousal and how children might be expected to react to them. Many different kinds of emotional patterns have been identified. For purposes here, we have arbitrarily selected for discussion the emotional states of fear, worry, anger, jealousy, and joy.

Fear

The term *fear* from the Old English *fir* may have been derived originally from the German word *fahr,* meaning danger or peril. In modern times fear is often thought of in terms of anxiety caused by present impending danger or peril. For example, one authoritative source[1] suggests that fear is generally defined as a normal and specific reaction to a genuine threat, which is present at the moment. Anxiety is usually defined as a more generalized reaction to a vague sense of threat in absence of a specific or realistic dangerous object. However, the terms are often used loosely and almost interchangeably. When fearful or anxious, individuals experience unpleasant changes in overt behavior, subjective feelings (including thoughts), and physiological activity.

Similarly, another source[2] contends that fears differ from anxiety in that the former are negative emotional responses to *specific* situations or objects, such as speaking before a group or receiving an injection, whereas the latter is an emotional state that tends to be prolonged and may be difficult to link to any specific environmental factor. But fears and anxiety are similar in the feelings they arouse: rapid heartbeat, sweating, quivering, heavy breathing, feeling weak or numb in the limbs, dizziness or faintness, muscular tension, the need to eliminate, and a sense of dread. Not all people experience all these signs of fear, but most experience some of them.

Fears are common among children, particularly in early childhood. Examples of such fears are fear of dogs, insects, the dark, and going to school. Childhood fears sometimes appear to be unexplainable and children have marked individual differences in susceptibility to fear. However, there is evidence that children display a definite tendency to learn adult's fears through identification with them or simply by observing them engage in fearful behavior. For example, if during a storm a child observes a parent being fearful, the child is likely to develop a similar fear and fear response pattern. On the other hand, childhood fears are a function of direct contact or experience with frightening events (e.g., if the child were attacked by a dog). Parental warnings, without the parent necessarily being fearful of such, about certain objects or events (e.g., "watch out for strangers," "stay away from fires") may also lead to developmental fears in children.

Children's fears often tend not to be taken seriously by adults, because some adults generally hold the belief that children's fears "will pass" or that they will "grow out of them." However, it has been found that this

---

[1]Whitehead, D'Ann, Shirley, Mariela and Walker, C. Eugene, Use of systematic desensitization in the treatment of children's fears, In *Stress in Childhood*, Ed. James H. Humphrey, New York, AMS Press, Inc. 1984, p. 213.

[2]Rathus, Spencer A., and Nevid, Jeffrey S. *Behavior Therapy*, New York, New American Library, 1977, p. 36.

may not always be the case, and that without treatment many fears may be maintained through adulthood.

It is possible that sometimes it is not necessarily the arousal itself but rather the way something is presented that determines whether there will be a fear reaction. For example, if a child is trying to perform a stunt and the discussion is in terms of "if you do it that way you will break your neck," it is possible a fear response will occur. This is one of the many reasons for using a positive approach in dealing with children.

A child may react to fear by withdrawing. With very young children, this may be in the form of crying or breath holding. With a child under three years of age (and in some older children as well), the "ostrich" approach may be used; that is, he may hide his face in order to get away from it. As children grow older, these forms of reactions may decrease or cease altogether because of social pressures. For instance, it may be considered "sissy" to cry, especially for boys. The validity of this kind of thinking is of course open to question.

Worry

This might be considered an imaginary form of fear and it can be a fear not aroused directly from the child's environment. Worry can be aroused by imagining a situation that could possibly arise; that is, a child could worry about not being able to perform well in a certain activity. Since worries are likely to be caused by imaginary rather than real conditions, they are not likely to be found in abundance among young children. Perhaps the reason for this is that a very young child has not reached the stage of intellectual development at which he or she might imagine certain things that could cause worry. While children will respond to worry in different ways, certain manifestitations such as nail biting may be symptomatic of this condition.

An interesting recent study[3] indicated that children in the 10–11 year age range worry most about the following.

1. AIDS
2. Drugs
3. Dying
4. Grades
5. Homework
6. Moving somewhere else

---

[3]The Mini Page, *The Washington Post*, December 25, 1988.

It is interesting to note that worry about AIDS and drugs has been prompted mainly by television comments about these subjects, and not necessarily because children have a personal awareness of them.

Anger

This emotional response tends to occur more frequently than that of fear. This is probably because there are more conditions that incite anger. In addition, some children quickly learn that anger may get attention that otherwise would not be forthcoming. It is likely that as children get older they may show more anger responses than fear responses because they soon see that there is not much to fear.

Anger is caused by many factors, one of which is interference with movements that a child may want to execute. This interference can come from others or by the child's own limitations in ability and physical development.

Because of individual differences of children, there is a wide variation in anger responses. These responses are either *impulsive* or *inhibited*. In impulsive responses, the child manifests an overt action either toward another person or an object that caused the anger. For instance, a child who collides with a door might take out the anger by kicking or hitting the door. (This form of child behavior is also sometimes manifested by some "adults.") Inhibited responses are likely to be kept under control, and as children mature emotionally, they acquire more ability to control their anger.

Jealousy

This response usually occurs when a child feels a threat of loss of affection. Many child psychologists believe that jealousy is closely related to anger. Because of this, the child may build up resentment against another person. Jealousy can be devastating in childhood and every effort should be made to avoid it.

Jealousy is concerned with social interaction that involves persons the child likes. These individuals can be parents, siblings, teachers, and peers. There are various ways in which the child may respond. These include: (1) being aggressive toward the one of whom one is jealous or possibly toward others as well, (2) withdrawing from the person whose affections he thinks have been lost, and (3) possible development of an "I don't care" attitude.

In some cases children will not respond in any of the above ways. They might try to excel over the person of whom they are jealous or they might tend to do things to impress the person whose affections they thought had been lost.

Joy

This pleasant emotion is one for which we strive because it is so important to maintaining emotional stability in children. Causes of joy differ from one age level to another and from one child to another at the same age level. This is to say that what might be joyful for one person might not necessarily be so for another.

Joy is expressed in various ways, but the most common are laughing and smiling, the latter being a restrained form of laughter. Some people respond to joy with a state of relaxation. This is difficult to detect, because it has little or no overt manifestations. Nevertheless, it may be noticed when one compares it with body tension caused by unpleasant emotion.

Factors That Influence Emotionality

If we can consider that a child is emotionally fit when his emotions are properly controlled and he is becoming emotionally mature, then emotional fitness is dependent to a certain extent upon certain factors that influence emotionality in childhood. The following is a description of some of these factors.

Fatigue

There are two types of fatigue: *acute* and *chronic.* Acute fatigue is a natural outcome of sustained severe exertion. It is due to physical factors such as the accumulation of the by-products of muscular exertion in the blood and to excessive *oxygen debt* — the ability of the body to take in as much oxygen as is being consumed by the muscular work. Psychological considerations may also be important in acute fatigue. That is, an individual who becomes bored with his work and who becomes preoccupied with the discomfort involved will become "fatigued" much sooner than if he is highly motivated to do the same work, is not bored, and does not think about the discomfort.

Chronic fatigue refers to fatigue that lasts over extended periods, in contrast to acute fatigue, which tends to be followed by a recovery phase and restoration to "normal" within a more or less brief period of time. Chronic fatigue may be due to any or a variety of medical conditions ranging from a disease to malnutrition. (Such conditions are the concern of the physician, who, incidentally, should evaluate all cases of chronic fatigue in order to assure that a disease condition is not responsible.) It may also be due to psychological factors such as extreme boredom and/or worry of having to do what one does not wish to do over an extended period.

Fatigue predisposes children to irritability; consequently, actions are taken to ward it off, such as having rest periods, or, in the case of nursery school, fruit juice periods. In this particular regard, some studies show that the hungrier a child is, the more prone he may be to outbursts of anger.

Inferior Health Status

The same thing holds true here as in the case of fatigue. Temporary poor health, such as colds and the like, tend to make children irritable. There are studies that show that there are fewer emotional outbursts among healthy than unhealthy children.

Intelligence

Studies tend to show that, on the average, children of low intelligence have less emotional control than children with higher levels of intelligence. This may be because there may be less frustration if a child is intelligent enough to figure things out. The reverse could also be true, because children with high levels of intelligence are better able to perceive things that would be likely to arouse emotions.

Social Environment

In a social environment where such things as quarreling and unrest exist, a child is predisposed to unpleasant emotional conditions. Likewise, school schedules that are too crowded can cause undue emotional excitation among children.

Family Relationships

There are a variety of conditions concerned with family relationships that can influence childhood emotionality. Among others, these include: (1) parental neglect, (2) overanxious parents, and (3) overprotective parents.

Aspiration Levels

It can make for an emotionally unstable situation if parent expectations are beyond a child's ability. In addition, children who have not been made aware of their own limitations may set goals too high and as a result have too many failures.

All of these factors can have a negative influence on childhood emotionality and, thus, possibly induce emotional stress. Therefore, efforts should be made as far as possible to eliminate the negative aspects of these factors. Those that cannot be completely eliminated should at least be kept under control.

EMOTIONAL NEEDS OF CHILDREN

Among the basic emotional needs of children are: (1) the need for a sense of security and trust, (2) the need for self-identity and self-respect, (3) the need for success, achievement and recognition, and (4) the need for independence.

Emotional maturity could be expressed in terms of the fulfillment of these general emotional needs. More specific emotional needs can be reflected in the developmental characteristics of growing children. A number of such emotional characteristics are identified in the following lists at the different age levels.

Five-Year-Old Children

1. Seldom shows jealousy toward younger siblings.
2. Usually sees only one way to do a thing.
3. Usually sees only one answer to a question.
4. Inclined not to change plans in the middle of an activity, but would rather begin over.
5. May fear being deprived of mother.
6. Some definite personality traits evidenced.
7. Is learning to get along better, but still may resort to quarreling and fighting.
8. Likes to be trusted with errands.
9. Enjoys performing simple tasks.
10. Wants to please and do what is expected of him.
11. Is beginning to sense right and wrong in terms of specific situations.

Six-Year-Old Children

1. Restless and may have difficulty in making decisions.
2. Emotional pattern of anger may be difficult to control at times.
3. Behavior patterns may often be explosive and unpredictable.
4. Jealousy toward siblings at times; at other times takes pride in siblings.
5. Greatly excited by anything new.
6. Behavior susceptible to shifts in direction, inwardly motivated and outwardly stimulated.
7. May be self-assertive and dramatic.

Seven-Year-Old Children

1. Curiosity and creative desires may condition responses.
2. May be difficult to take criticism from adults.
3. Wants to be more independent.
4. Reaching for new experiences and trying to relate himself to enlarged world.
5. Overanxious to reach goals set by parents and teachers.
6. Critical to himself and sensitive to failure.
7. Emotional pattern of anger is more controlled.
8. Becoming less impulsive and boisterous in actions than at six.

Eight-Year-Old Children

1. Dislikes taking much criticism from adults.
2. Can give and take criticism in his own group.
3. May develop enemies.
4. Does not like to be treated as a child.
5. Has a marked sense of humor.
6. First impulse is to blame others.
7. Becoming more realistic and wants to find out for himself.

Nine-Year-Old Children

1. May sometimes be outspoken and critical of the adults he knows, although he has a genuine fondness for them.

2. Responds best to adults who treat him as an individual and approach him in an adult way.
3. Likes recognition for what he has done and responds well to deserved praise.
4. Likely to be backward about public recognition, but likes private praise.
5. Developing sympathy and loyalty to others.
6. Does not mind criticism or punishment if he thinks it is fair, but is indignant if he thinks it is unfair.
7. Disdainful of danger to and safety of himself, which may be a result of increasing interest in activities involving challenges.

Ten-Year-Old Children

1. Increasing tendency to rebel against adult domination.
2. Capable of loyalties and hero worship, and he can inspire it in his schoolmates.
3. Can be readily inspired to group loyalties in his club organization.
4. Likes the sense of solidarity that comes from keeping a group secret as a member of a group.
5. Each sex has an increasing tendency to show lack of sympathy and understanding with the other.
6. Boys' and girls' behavior and interests becoming increasingly different.

Eleven-Year-Old Children

1. If unskilled in group games and game skills, he may tend to withdraw.
2. Boys may be concerned if they feel they are underdeveloped.
3. May appear to be indifferent and uncooperative.
4. Moods change quickly.
5. Wants to grow up, but may be afraid to leave childhood security behind.
6. Increase in self-direction and in a serious attitude toward work.
7. Need for approval to feel secure.
8. Beginning to have a fully developed idea of own importance.

Twelve-Year-Old Children

1. Beginning to develop a truer picture of morality.
2. Clearer understanding of real causal relations.
3. The process of sexual maturation involves structural and physiological changes with possible perplexing and disturbing emotional problems.
4. Personal appearance may become a source of great conflict, and learning to appreciate good grooming or the reverse may be prevalent.
5. May be very easily hurt when criticized or made the scapegoat.
6. Maladjustment may occur when there is not a harmonious relationship between child and adults.

The above emotional characteristics reflect some of the emotional needs of children at the different age levels; and these characteristics should be taken into account in the school environment if we expect to meet with success in our efforts to help children develop emotionally.

GUIDELINES FOR EMOTIONAL DEVELOPMENT OF CHILDREN

It is imperative to set forth some guidelines for emotional development if we are to meet with any degree of success in our attempts to provide for emotional development of children. The reason for this is to assure, at least to some extent, that our efforts in attaining optimum emotional development will be based upon a scientific approach. These guidelines might well be taken in the form of *concepts of emotional development.* This approach enables us to give serious consideration to what is known about how children grow and develop. The following list of concepts of emotional development is submitted with this general idea in mind.

1. *An emotional response may be brought about by a goal's being furthered or thwarted.* The teacher should make a very serious effort to assure successful experiences for every child. This can be accomplished in part by attempting to provide for individual differences within given school experiences. The school setting should be such that each child derives a feeling of personal worth through making some sort of positive contribution.

2. *Self-realization experiences should be constructive.* The opportunity

for creative experiences that afford the child a chance for self-realization should be inherent in school. Teachers might well consider planning with children to see that all school activities are meeting their needs and, as a result, involve constructive experiences.

3. *Emotional responses increase as the development of the child brings greater awareness and the ability to remember the past and to anticipate the future.* In the school setting the teacher can remind the children of their past pleasant emotional responses with words of praise. This could encourage children to repeat such responses later in similar situations and thus provide a better learning situation.

4. *As the child develops, the emotional reactions tend to become less violent and more discriminating.* A well-planned program of school experiences and wholesome home activities should be such that it provides for release of aggression in a socially acceptable manner.

5. *Emotional reactions tend to increase beyond normal expectancy toward the constructive or destructive reactions on the balance of furthering or hindering experience of the child.* For some children the confidence they need to be able to face the problems of life may come through physical expression. Therefore, experiences such as good physical education programs in the schools have tremendous potential to help contribute toward a solid base of total development.

6. *Depending on certain factors, a child's own feelings may be accepted or rejected by the individual.* Children's school experiences should make them feel good and have confidence in themselves. Satisfactory self-concept is closely related to body control; physical activity-oriented experiences might be considered as one of the best ways of contributing to it. Therefore, it is important to consider those kinds of experiences for children that will provide them with the opportunity for a certain degree of freedom of movement.

OPPORTUNITIES FOR EMOTIONAL DEVELOPMENT IN THE SCHOOL ENVIRONMENT

The school has the potential to provide for emotional stability. The extent to which this actually occurs is dependent primarily on the kind of emotional climate provided by the teacher. For this reason, it appears pertinent to examine some of the potential opportunities that exist for emotional development in the school situation. It should be borne in mind that these opportunities will not accrue automatically, but that teachers need to work constantly to try to make such conditions a reality.

1. *Release of aggression in a socially acceptable manner.* This appears to be an outstanding way in which school activities such as physical education can help to make children more secure and emotionally stable. For example, kicking a ball in a game of kickball, batting a softball, or engaging in a combative stunt can afford a socially acceptable way of releasing aggression.

2. *Inhibition of direct response of unpleasant emotions.* This statement does not necessarily mean that feelings concerned with such unpleasant emotions as fear and anger should be completely restrained. On the contrary, the interpretation should be that such feelings can take place less frequently in a wholesome school environment. This means that opportunities should be provided to relieve tension rather than aggravate it.

3. *Promotion of pleasant emotions.* Perhaps there is too much concern with suppressing unpleasant emotions and not enough attention given to promoting the pleasant ones. This means that the school should provide a range of activities by which all children can succeed. Thus, all children, regardless of ability, should be afforded the opportunity for success, at least some of the time.

4. *Recognition of one's abilities and limitations.* It has already been mentioned that a wide range of activities should provide an opportunity for success for all. This should make it easier in the school setting to provide for individual differences of children so that all of them can progress within the limits of their own skill and ability.

5. *Understanding about the ability and achievement of others.* In the school experience emphasis can be placed upon achievements of the group, along with the function of each individual in the group. Team play and group effort is important in most school situations.

6. *Being able to make a mistake without being ostracized.* In the school setting this requires that the teacher serve as a catalyst who helps children understand the idea of trial and error. Emphasis can be placed on *trying* and on the fact that one can learn not only from his own mistakes but also from the mistakes of others.

This discussion has included just a few examples of the numerous opportunities to help provide for emotional development in the school environment. The resourceful and creative teacher should be able to expand this list manyfold.

IMPLICATIONS OF RESEARCH IN
EMOTIONAL BEHAVIOR OF CHILDREN

Over the years, attempts have been made to study various aspects of childhood emotions. One such undertaking was that of the National Institute of Education mentioned in the preceding chapter. The following is a list of generalizations derived from the findings of this study as it pertains to *aggression* in children. It is accompanied by possible general implications for the school environment.

1. *Children rewarded for aggression learn that aggression pays off.* This generalization is concerned with the extent to which a teacher uses praise for achievement. The teacher must be able to discern quickly whether success was due more to aggressive behavior than skill or ability. The important thing here is the extent of aggressive behavior. Certainly, a teacher should not thwart enthusiasm. It is sometimes difficult to determine whether an act was due to genuine enthusiasm or to overt, undesirable, aggressive behavior.

2. *Children involved in constructive activities may be less likely to behave aggressively.* In the school setting, this implies that lessons should be well-planned so that time is spent on constructive learning activities. When this is accomplished, it will be more likely that desirable and worthwhile learning will take place.

3. *Children who have alternative responses readily available are less likely to resort to aggression to get what they want.* This is concerned essentially with teacher-child relationships. While the school environment involves group situations, there are many "one-on-one" opportunities between teacher and child. This gives the teacher a chance to verbalize to the child the kind of behavior that is expected under certain conditions. For example, a child who *asks* for an object such as a ball is more likely to receive cooperation. A child who *grabs* an object is more likely to elicit retaliatory aggression. Teaching reinforcement can increase children's use of nonaggressive solutions to interpersonal problems. The teacher should be ready to intervene in a potentially aggressive situation before aggression occurs, encouraging children to use nonaggressive methods to solve conflicts. The teacher can provide verbal alternatives for those children who do not think of them. For example, "I am playing with this now," or "You can ask him to trade with you."

4. *Children imitate behavior of people they like, and they often adopt a teacher's behavior.* Teachers are more likely to be a model adopted by

children than would be the case of other adults, sometimes including parents. One of the reasons is that many children like to try to please their teachers and tend to make serious efforts to do so. Of course, it is helpful if a teacher is nonaggressive in his or her own behavior.

5. *Cooperation may be incompatible with aggression.* This could be interpreted to mean that a teacher should consistently attend to and reinforce all cooperative behavior. Children consistently reinforced for cooperative behavior are likely to increase cooperative interactions while simultaneously decreasing aggressive behavior.

EVALUATING INFLUENCES OF THE SCHOOL ENVIRONMENT ON EMOTIONAL DEVELOPMENT

What we are essentially concerned with here is how an individual teacher can make some sort of valid evaluation of the extent to which the school environment is contributing to emotional development. This means that the teacher should make some attempt to assess school experiences with reference to whether or not these experiences are providing for emotional maturity.

One approach would be to refer back to the list of opportunities for emotional development in the school environment suggested previously. These opportunities have been converted into a rating scale as follows and may be used by the teacher.

1. The school experiences provide for release of aggression in a socially acceptable manner.
   4 most of the time
   3 some of the time
   2 occasionally
   1 infrequently
2. The school experiences provide for inhibition of direct response to unpleasant emotions.
   4 most of the time
   3 some of the time
   2 occasionally
   1 infrequently
3. The school experiences provide for promotion of pleasant emotions.
   4 most of the time
   3 some of the time

2 occasionally

1 infrequently

4. The school experiences provide for recognition of one's abilities and limitations.

   4 most of the time

   3 some of the time

   2 occasionally

   1 infrequently

5. The school experiences provide for an understanding about the ability and achievement of others.

   4 most of the time

   3 some of the time

   2 occasionally

   1 infrequently

6. The school experiences provide for being able to make a mistake without being ostracized.

   4 most of the time

   3 some of the time

   2 occasionally

   1 infrequently

If a teacher makes these ratings objectively and conscientiously, a reasonably good procedure for evaluation is provided. Ratings can be made periodically to see if positive changes appear to be taking place. Ratings can be made for a single experience, a group of experiences, or for the total school environment. This procedure can help the teacher identify the extent to which school experiences and/or conditions under which the experiences take place are contributing to emotional development.

Chapter 6

INTELLECTUAL DEVELOPMENT

INTELLECTUAL NEEDS OF CHILDREN

Satisfactorily meeting children's intellectual needs is one of our greatest concerns, as it is of paramount importance to success in school and life in general. In Chapter 1 we identified some *general* intellectual needs of children as: (1) a need for challenging experiences at the child's level of ability; (2) a need for intellectually successful and satisfying experiences; (3) a need for the opportunity to solve problems; and (4) a need for the opportunity to participate in creative experiences instead of always having to conform.

As in the case of physical, social, and emotional needs, children have certain *specific* intellectual needs. The specific needs can be reflected in the developmental characteristics of children. A number of intellectual characteristics are identified in the following lists at the different age levels.

Five-Year-Old Children

1. Enjoys copying designs, letters, and numbers.
2. Interested in completing tasks.
3. May tend to monopolize table conversation.
4. Memory for past events good.
5. Looks at books and pretends to read; in fact, some are beginning to read at this level.
6. Likes recordings, words, and music that tell a story.
7. Enjoys counting objects.
8. Over 2,000 words in speaking vocabulary.
9. Can speak in complete sentences.
10. Can sing simple melodies, beat good rhythms, and recognize simple tunes.
11. Daydreams seem to center around make-believe play.
12. Attention span increasing up to twenty minutes in some cases.

13. Is able to plan activities.
14. Enjoys stories, dramatic plays, and poems.
15. Enjoys making up dances to music.
16. Pronunciation is usually clear.
17. Can express his needs well in words.

Six-Year-Old Children

1. Speaking vocabulary of over 2,500 words.
2. Interest span inclined to be short.
3. Knows number combinations up to ten.
4. Knows comparative values of the common coins.
5. Can define objects in terms of what they are for.
6. Knows right and left side of body.
7. Has an association with creative activity and motorized life experience.
8. Drawings are crude but realistic and suggestive of early man.
9. Will contribute to guided group planning.
10. Conversation usually concerns his own experience and interests.
11. Curiosity is active and memory is strong.
12. Identifies himself with imaginary characters.

Seven-Year-Old Children

1. Abstract thinking is starting to begin.
2. Is able to listen longer.
3. Reads some books by himself.
4. Is able to reason, but has little experience upon which to base judgments.
5. The attention span is still short and retention poor, but does not object to repetition.
6. Reaction time is still slow.
7. Learning to evaluate the achievements of self and others.
8. Concerned with own lack of skill and achievements.
9. Becoming more realistic and less imaginative.

Eight-Year-Old Children

1. Can tell day of month and year.
2. Voluntary attention span increasing.

3. Interested in far-off places, and ways of communication now have real meaning.
4. Becoming more aware of adult world and his place in it.
5. Ready to take on almost anything.
6. Shows a capacity for self-evaluation.
7. Likes to memorize.
8. Not always very good at telling time, but very much aware of it.

Nine-Year-Old Children

1. Individual differences are clear and distinct.
2. Some real interests are beginning to develop.
3. Beginning to have a strong sense of right and wrong.
4. Understands explanations.
5. Interests are closer to ten or eleven year olds than to seven or eight year olds.
6. As soon as a project fails to hold interest, it may be dropped without further thought.
7. Attention span is greatly increased.
8. Seems to be guided best by a reason, simple, and clear-cut, for a decision that needs to be made.
9. Ready to learn from occasional failure of his judgment as long as learning takes place in situations where failure will not have too serious consequences.
10. Able to make up own mind and come to decisions.
11. Marked reading disabilities begin to be more evident and may tend to influence the personality.
12. Range of interest in reading in that many are great readers while others may be barely interested in books.
13. Will average between six and seven words per remark.

Ten-Year-Old Children

1. Works with executive speed and some like the challenge of arithmetic.
2. Shows a capacity to budget his time and energy.
3. Can attend to a visual task and at the same time maintain conversation.
4. Some become discouraged and may give up trying when unsuccessful.

5. The attention span has lengthened considerably, with the child able to listen to and follow directions and retain knowledge more easily.
6. Beginning understanding of real causal relations.
7. Making finer conceptual distinctions and thinking reflectively.
8. Developing a scientific approach.
9. Better oriented with respect to time.
10. Ready to plan his day and accept responsibility for getting things done on time.

Eleven-Year-Old Children

1. Increasing power of attention and abstract reasoning.
2. Able to maintain a longer period of intellectual activity between firsthand experiences.
3. Interested in scientific experiments and procedures.
4. Can carry on many individual intellectual responsibilities.
5. Able to discuss problems and to see different sides of questions.
6. May lack maturity of judgment.
7. Increased language facility.
8. Attention span is increasing, and concentration may be given to a task for a long period of time.
9. Level of aspiration has increased.
10. Growing in ability to use several facts to make a decision.
11. Insight into causal relationships is developing more and is manifested by many how and why questions.

Twelve-Year-Old Children

1. Learns more ways of studying and controlling the physical world.
2. Uses language (on many occasions his own vocabulary) to exchange ideas for explanatory reasons.
3. More use of reflective thinking and greater ease of distinction.
4. Continuation in development of scientific approach.

It should be obvious that the above intellectual characteristics of children of different ages should be taken into account if we are to meet with any degree of success in our efforts in the direction of intellectual development.

GUIDELINES FOR INTELLECTUAL DEVELOPMENT

Guidelines for intellectual development are set forth here in the same manner that guidelines for physical, social, and emotional development were proposed in previous chapters; that is, these guidelines take the form of valid *concept of intellectual development.* When we have some sort of basis for intellectual behavior of children as they grow and develop, we are then in a better position to provide school experiences that are likely to be compatible with intellectual development. The following list of concepts of intellectual development are submitted with this general idea in mind.

1. *Children differ in intelligence.* Teachers should be aware that poor performance of some children might be due to the fact that they have difficulty with communication. Differences in intelligence levels need to be taken into account in the planning of lessons. To meet this need, some elementary schools departmentalize classes for the basic subjects of reading and mathematics.

2. *Mental development is rapid in early childhood and slows down later.* Children want and need challenging kinds of experiences at all grade levels.

3. *Intelligence develops through interaction of the child and his environment.* Experiences should involve a process of interaction with the environment. There are many problem-solving opportunities in the well-planned class environment, and thus the child can be presented with challenging learning situations.

4. *Emotional stress may affect measures of intelligence.* Experiences should have potential value in the relief of emotional stress. This can possibly make the child more effective from an intellectual point of view. (This subject will be discussed in greater detail in Chapter 7.)

5. *Extremes in intelligence show differences in personality characteristics.* The teacher should be aware of the range of intelligence of children in a particular group. Experiences should be provided that challenge the so-called gifted child as well as meeting the needs of those children who are below average. Children should learn to respect individual differences as far as levels of intelligence are concerned.

6. *The child's self-concept of his ability to deal with intellectual tasks influences his successful dealing with such tasks.* Experiences must contain a large degree of variation. This way it will likely insure that all children will achieve success at one time or another.

SLOW LEARNING CHILDREN

The basic principle of *teaching to the individual differences of the learner* has led to the development of many components within the educational system. Programs and services that reflect the needs of those with widely varying abilities are available in most school systems.

Within this broad concept of educational opportunities there has developed a national concern in recent years for the problems of children with learning impairment. Direct grants for research and service for these children have enabled government agencies and private foundations to work cooperatively to help the schools do a better job, both in identifying these children and providing more appropriate learning environments for them. The neurologist, the physician, the psychologist, and the researcher in education are contributing new insights into working with these children.

Some of the research in ways children with mental deficits and impairment learn provides the teacher with useful guidelines. Research has been directed not only to the etiology, the nature, and the degree of learning impairment, but also to the educational environment within which learning takes place for children with such impairments.

Identifying the Slow Learner

While there has been agreement that the needs of children with learning impairment must be reflected in appropriate teaching techniques, there is an increasing awareness of the problems of identification. Too many children in our classrooms have been mistaken for slow learners because of their difficulties in mastering such academic skills as reading and mathematics. It is essential, therefore, that there can be a clear understanding of basic differences among children with the *slow learner syndrome*, but whose learning problems may be caused by factors other than subnormal intellectual functioning. With this general frame of reference in mind, the subsequent discussions will focus upon slow learners classified as (1) the child with mental retardation, (2) the child with depressed potential, and (3) the child with a learning disability.

The Child with Mental Retardation

In the literature the broad generic term *mentally retarded* encompasses all degrees of mental deficit. The designation of the term *slow learner* has been given to those children who have a mild degree (along a continuum) of subnormal intellectual functioning as measured by intelligence tests. The intelligence quotients of these children fall within the range of 70 or 75 to 90. This child in the classroom is making average or below average progress in the academic skills, depending where he falls along the continuum of mental retardation. He will probably demonstrate slowness in learning such academic skills as reading and possibly mathematics. He will very likely have difficulty in the area of more complex mental processes of defining, analyzing, and comparing. He tends to be a poor reasoner. However, he need not necessarily be equally slow in all aspects of behavior. He may be above average in social adaptability or artistic endeavors.

In respect to physical characteristics, personality, and adjustment, slow-learning children are as variable and heterogeneous as children in the average and above-average range of intellectual potential. Attributes often identified with slow learners are laziness, inattention, and short attention span. However, these characteristics are likely to be eliminated when the educational environment is geared to the needs of children and when there is appropriateness, meaningfulness, and purposefulness to the learning activity.

There is some variance in the literature as to whether these children should be identified as mentally retarded. There is general agreement that the slow learner represents a mild degree of subnormal intellectual functioning, whether or not he is labeled mentally retarded. A good many years ago Kirk[1] accurately described the characteristic educational life patterns of those within the broad educational categories of subnormal intelligence, namely (a) the slow learner, (b) the educable mentally retarded, (c) the trainable mentally retarded, and (d) the totally dependent mentally retarded. With reference to the slow learner it is suggested that this type of child is not considered mentally retarded because he is able to achieve a moderate degree of academic success even though at a slower rate than the average child. He is educated in the regular class program without special provisions except an adaptation of the regular class program to fit his slower learning ability. At the adult level he is usually self-supporting, independent, and socially adjusted.

In the last two decades the dimension of social adaptiveness has gained as an influencing criterion for identification of the mentally

---

[1]Kirk, Samuel A., *Educating Exceptional Children*, Boston, Houghton-Mifflin, 1962, pp. 85–86.

retarded. For example, Dywab[2] emphasized the criterion of *social acceptance* in terms of the growing reluctance to identify persons as mentally retarded on the basis of intellectualy subnormality alone.

Thus, a person who scores 65 on an intelligence test and who at the same time shows himself well able to adapt to the social demands of his particular environment at home, at work, and in the community should not necessarily be considered retarded. Indeed, it is now known that he is not generally so considered.

It is apparent, therefore, that the slow learner with whom the teacher may be working in the classroom may have significant intellectual subnormality.

The Child with Depressed Potential

For some years it has been recognized that factors other than intellectual subnormality affected achievement in the classroom. Concern in our schools today for the disadvantaged and culturally different children is placing increased emphasis on an understanding of these factors. The groundwork was laid several decades ago when these factors were considered by Featherstone[3] in his delineation of the limited educational achievement of the *constitutional slow learner* with subnormal intellectual capacity from the *functional slow learner*. The latter is often mistaken by teachers for a slow learner with limited potential because he is having difficulty achieving in the classroom. He may be making limited progress in acquiring the academic skills or he may be a behavior problem, but his limited achievements are caused by numerous other factors that serve to depress an individual's ability to learn. Such factors may be the lack of psychosocial stimulation from limited socioeconomic environment, inadequate hearing and vision, emotional problems in relationships with family and peers, malnutrition or poor general health. It is important to recognize that the situation is not necessarily permanent. Both educational programs and conditions affecting the child's physical, social, emotional, and intellectual well-being can be improved.

The Child with a Learning Disability

A further compounding of the problem of identification of the *slow learner* has occurred with studies of children who do not come under the

---

[2]Dywab, Gunnar, Who are the mentally retarded? *Children*, 15–44, 1968.

[3]Featherstone, W. B., Teaching the slow learner In Caswell, Hollis L., (Ed.), *Practical Suggestions for Teaching*, 2nd ed., New York, Teachers College, Columbia University, 1951, No 1, pp 10–11.

categories of the *constitutional* or *functional slow learner,* but whose class-room achievement may be similar. Often the learning disabled child is called stupid or lazy, or both. In fact, he is neither, and such labels can have a negative influence on learning as well as self-concept.

The research identifying learning-disability children indicates that their learning has been impaired in specific areas of verbal and/or nonverbal learning, but their *potential* for learning is categorized as normal or above. Thus, these learning-disability children fall within the 90 and above IQ range in either the verbal or nonverbal areas. Total IQ is not used as the criterion for determining learning potential inasmuch as adequate intelligence, either verbal or nonverbal, may be obscured in cases where the total IQ falls below 90, but in which specific aspects of intelligence fall within the definition of adequate intelligence. The learning-disability child whose IQ falls below the normal range, and where a learning disability is present is considered to have a multiple involvement.

In learning-disability children there are deficits in verbal and/or nonverbal learning. There may be impairment of expressive, receptive, or integrative functions. There is concern for deficits in the function of input and output, of sensory modalities, and of degree of impairment.

The learning-disability child shows marked differences from the child with limited potential. There are both qualitative and quantitative differences. The learning-disability child has more potential for learning. The means by which he learns are different.

While there may be some overlapping in the educational methods used with these three groups identified as *slow learners,* there obviously must be differentiation in educational goals and approaches for these various groups. Correct identification of the factors causing *slowness in learning* is essential in teaching with the individual differences among children.

Learning Characteristics of the Slow Learner

When considering educational processes that would provide a success-ful learning experience for children with limited intellectual potential, it is necessary to examine some of their basic characteristics of learning as found from numerous studies. *Slow learners* appear to follow the same patterns as those who have more adequate intellectual endowment in terms of the sequence of growth and development. The basic difference is the time schedule at which these children arrive at various levels of development. Theoretically, the child with an IQ of 80 develops intellectually at a rate only four-fifths that of the average child. The rate of development of these children is more closely correlated with their mental age than their chronological age.

Differences have been found in comparison of the learning process in mathematics and reading of the mentally retarded and normal children. However, these differences are not necessarily attributable to *ability* to learn, but perhaps more to the influence of teaching methods. Included among the factors affecting the learning process are the value systems of the individual and his own concept of self as a learner. These two factors must be recognized as particularly important. The reason for this is that there are so many negative psychosocial factors operating within the life space of large percentages of the mentally retarded who can maintain themselves only in a low socioeconomic environment.

GIFTED AND TALENTED CHILDREN

When we get into any kind of labeling in education we have problems, not only with communication with individuals outside a given field but also with workers in the field itself. This seems to be the case with the terms *gifted* and *talented* because there is still a fair amount of disagreement among professionals themselves regarding the meaning of these terms.

Definitions of giftedness in the mid 1900s focused on IQ or intellectual ability as the main indicator of giftedness. The gifted individual was viewed as one possessing a high level of intelligence, which, in turn, was seen as a fixed and measurable quantity. Correspondingly, the gifted child could be easily defined as a person with an IQ of at or above an established point.[4] (Some current estimates suggest that gifted students with IQs of 130 and above comprise about 3 percent of the school population.) The fact that this situation is still somewhat widespread today is shown in a recent study[5] that revealed that dependence upon measures of cognitive ability are the prevailing identification tools used in selecting pupils for programs for the gifted and/or talented. Although achievement tests appeared to have replaced IQ tests as keystone instru-

---

[4]Alexander, Patricia A., and Muia, Joseph A., *Gifted Education*, Rockville, Maryland, Aspen Systems Corporation, 1982, p. 10.

[5]Yarborough, Betty H., and Johnson, Roger, A., Identifying the gifted: A theory-practice gap, *Gifted Child Quarterly*, Summer 1983.

ments, they reflect an academic posture similar to that of IQ tests and support the intellectual aura characteristic of programs for the gifted/talented historically evident in this century. In other words, they sample extant knowledge or skills—perhaps to a degree even greater than IQ tests. Over 90 percent of the programs identified gifted with achievement tests and almost 75 percent used IQ tests for this purpose. This finding tends to contradict the current popular rhetoric which recommends that behavioral data replace the role of hardline cognitive test scores as a means of identifying gifted children.

It is interesting to note that the terms *gifted* and *talented* are often defined in combination. Traditionally, as mentioned above, giftedness has been associated with extraordinary intellectual ability, and there are many persons who have high levels of intelligence who also display special talent. However, on the contrary, one could have a special talent and at the same time have so-called normal intelligence.

In this general regard, it is interesting to note that the United States Congress in passing legislation authorizing allocations of funds for education of the gifted used a broad definition suggested by a special study on the status of education of the gifted in this country.[6] This study reported that gifted and talented children are those identified by professionally qualified persons who by virtue of outstanding abilities are capable of high performance. These are children who require differentiated educational programs and/or services beyond those normally provided by the regular school program in order to realize their contributions to self and society. Children capable of high performance include those with demonstrated achievement and/or potential ability in any of the following areas, singly or in combination.

1. General intellectual ability.
2. Specific academic aptitude.
3. Creative or productive thinking.
4. Leadership ability.
5. Visual and performing arts.
6. Psychomotor ability.

It was assumed that utilization of these criteria for identification of the gifted and talented would encompass a minimum of 3 to 5 percent of the total school population. (Incidentally, it was recently indicated that only

---

[6]Marland, Sidney P., Jr., *Education of the Gifted and Talented*, Report to the United States Congress by the Commissioner of Education, Washington, DC, U. S. Department of Health, Education and Welfare, 1971.

about one-half of the gifted children in this country have been identified as such, and that only about one-third are being served by special school programs.) In any event, the *Gifted and Talented Children's Education Act of 1978* utilized the following description: "Gifted and talented children means children and, where applicable, youth, who are identified at the preschool, elementary, or secondary level as possessing demonstrated potential abilities that give evidence of high performance capability in areas such as intellectual, creative, specific academic, or leadership ability, or in the performing and visual arts, and who by reason thereof, require services or activities not ordinarily provided by the school."

Later, the language used in P.L. 97-35, the *Education Consolidation and Improvement Act,* passed by Congress in 1981 was: "Gifted and talented children are now referred to as children who give evidence of high performance capability in areas such as intellectual, creative, artistic, leadership capacity, or specific academic fields, and who require services or activities not ordinarily provided by the school in order to fully develop such capabilities."

It should be readily discerned that all of the language used in the above descriptions is characterized more by likeness than by difference. Moreover, the above focuses on those more or less positive traits and characteristics of gifted children.

One well-known authority on the subject, Virginia Ehrlich,[7] suggests that besides identifying gifted children by means of known positive traits, the teacher should reevaluate the child who shows the following *negative* characteristics that may be clues to unrecognized giftedness.

1. Excessive restlessness or diagnosed hyperactivity.
2. Mischief making, especially if it is associated with a sharp sense of humor.
3. Poor achievement, even though other behavior contradicts this evidence.
4. Leadership as recognized by peers, for example, leading a gang.
5. Withdrawal, indifference, inattention, daydreaming in class.
6. Excessive cutting (skipping school).
7. Unwillingness to do homework.
8. Persistence in pursuing a discussion or topic beyond the teacher's expressed cutoff point.

---

[7]Ehrlich, Virginia Z., *Gifted Children: A Guide for Parents and Teachers,* Englewood Cliffs, NJ, Prentice-Hall, Inc., 1982, p. 164.

We hasten to mention that the above should not be interpreted to mean that gifted children are necessarily behavior problems. On the contrary, some research has shown that gifted elementary school students show fewer behavior problems than their nongifted classmates.[8]

Since intellectual ability still appears to be the primary attribute as far as gifted children are concerned, it seems important to comment further on this. It has been suggested by representatives of the *American Association for Gifted Children*[9] that generally the following evidence would indicate special intellectual gifts or talents.

1. Consistently very superior scores on many appropriate standardized tests.
2. Demonstration of advanced skills, imaginative thought, and intense interest and involvement.
3. Judgment of teachers, administrators, supervisors, and specialists in various fields, including the arts, who are familiar with the abilities and potential of the individual and are qualified to evaluate them.

An approach that we personally believe has merit is one concerned with acquiring knowledge of the intellectual traits and characteristics of the so-called normal child. With such information teachers and parents as well can determine to some degree the extent to which a given child may be above normal. (See lists of intellectual characteristics presented previously in this chapter.)

As mentioned elsewhere these intellectual characteristics have been developed through a documentary analysis of over a score of sources that have appeared in the literature in recent years. It should be understood that these intellectual characteristics are suggestive of the behavior patterns of the so-called normal child. This implies that if a child does not conform to these characteristics, it should not be interpreted to mean that he or she is seriously deviated from the normal. In other words, it should be recognized that each child progresses at his or her own rate and there is much overlapping of the characteristics at each of the age levels. It is reiterated that with the above information the reader should be in a better position to identify children who might be gifted when

---

[8]Ludwig, Gretchen and Cullinan, Douglas, Behavior problems of gifted and nongifted elementary school boys and girls, *Gifted Child Quarterly*, Winter 1984.

[9]Tannenbaum, Abraham J., and Neuman, Elizabeth, *Reaching Out: Advocacy for the Gifted and Talented*, American Association for Gifted Children, Teachers College, Columbia University, New York, 1980.

they behave intellectually in a way that is appreciably above that of the average child.

In closing this chapter we want to caution that as most of the readers are aware, an extremely high IQ does not necessarily guarantee success in the classroom. In our own work,[10] as well as that of others in the area of childhood stress, it has been demonstrated time and again that children who come from families in stress have difficulty coping with stress themselves. Sometimes this inability to cope has resulted in a child scoring several points lower on an intelligence test than would otherwise be the case. Therefore, it is possible that in those schools where IQ tests are the sole means used for determining placement of children in special programs for the gifted, children with stressful personal and family lives are being placed in programs below their potential. With good stress management for these children a "normal" child actually may turn out to be gifted. (The following chapter will go into a detailed discussion of childhood stress.)

In addition, some children with an extremely high IQ may suffer from certain kinds of learning disabilities that inhibit their ability to develop skills and concepts even at the average level. While this population is estimated at only 5 to 8 percent, these children experience much more trauma than the so-called normal child when a learning disability is present. As we have mentioned, children with learning disabilities are difficult to identify; that is, with traditional procedures. The "normal" gifted child is frequently overlooked on group-administered tests; in fact, it has been indicated that up to 70 percent of gifted children may not be identified if only group tests are used. Gifted children with learning disabilities perform very poorly on these group tests, especially when their deficiency is in the area of visual perception and they cannot read with understanding. It is even more critical that these children be given individually-administered tests than the "normal" gifted child. Not only will individual testing indicate their high intelligence, but it will also point out the area in which learning disabilities exist, such as perceptual and/or motor.[11]

Finally, another consideration that might be addressed is the person with a below-normal IQ who might be gifted, at least in some way. As an

---

[10]Humphrey, James H., and Humphrey, Joy N., *Controlling Stress in Children*, Springfield, Illinois, Charles C Thomas, Publisher, 1985.

[11]Elkind, Joel, The gifted child with learning disabilities, *Gifted Child Quarterly*, Summer 1983.

extreme example, take the case of an *idiot savant*. Thirteen-year-old John has an IQ of 61 and his reading has never progressed beyond third-grade level and his mathematics is limited to simple addition and subtraction. He is mentally retarded in every area but one, where he shines like a genius. At age eight he worked out a system of mental calendar-calculations, but he has such difficulty in speaking that psychologists can only guess at his method. He apparently works from a series of base dates as landmarks, counting backward or forward to reach the desired date. For two years past John can name the dates and days of the week instantaneously. For earlier years it will take him from 30 to 60 seconds.[12]

Psychologists have puzzled over the idiot savant for years. Some say that these people have defective abstract reasoning ability and must rely only on concrete thought processes. Others theorize that idiot savants are the product of their families and early environments.

---

[12]Making a savant, *Human Behavior*, March/April, 1973.

Chapter 7

STRESS AS A FACTOR IN CHILD DEVELOPMENT

Although we tend to think of undesirable stress as being mainly concerned with adults, there is plenty of evidence to demonstrate that it can have a devastating effect on developing children. There is no question about it, stress can take a tremendous toll on the physical, social, emotional, and intellectual development of children. It is the purpose of this chapter to examine various aspects of childhood stress that can impact upon child development.

As children begin the various stages of development, many are beset with problems of stress. The very first stage of child development, the period from birth to about 15 months, is considered to be the "intake" stage, because behavior and growth are characterized by *taking in*. This not only applies to food but to other things, such as sound, light, and the various forms of total care. At this early stage in the child's life *separation anxiety* can begin. Since the child is entirely dependent on the mother or other caregiver to meet its needs, separation may be seen as being deprived of these important needs. It is at this stage that the child's overseer—ordinarily the parent—should try to maintain a proper balance between meeting the child's needs and "overgratification." Many child development experts seem to agree that children who experience some stress from separation or for having to wait for a need to be fulfilled are gaining the opportunity to organize their psychological resources and adapt to stress. On the contrary, children who did not have this balance may tend to disorganize under stress.

During the stage from about 15 months to three years, children are said to develop autonomy. This can be described as the "I am what I can do" stage. Autonomy develops because most children can now move about rather easily. The child does not have to rely entirely on a caregiver to meet every single need. Autonomy also results from the development of mental processes, because the child can think about things and put language to use.

It is during this stage that the process of toilet training can be a major stressor. Children are not always given the needed opportunity to express autonomy during this process. It can be a difficult time for the child, because he or she is ordinarily expected to cooperate with, and gain the approval of, the principal caregiver. If the child cooperates and uses the toilet, approval is forthcoming; however, some autonomy is lost. If the child does not cooperate, disapproval may result. If this conflict is not resolved satisfactorily, some clinical psychologists believe it will emerge during adulthood in the form of highly anxious and compulsive behaviors.

The next stage, from three to five years, can be described as "I am what I think I am." Skills of body movement are being used in a more purposeful way. Children develop the ability to daydream and make believe, and these are used to manifest some of their behaviors. Pretending allows them to be what they want to be—anything from astronauts to zebras. It is possible, however, that resorting to too much fantasy may result in stress, because the children may become scared of their own fantasies.

Unquestionably children at all the early age levels, beginning at birth (and possibly before as well), are likely to encounter a considerable amount of stress in our complex modern society. The objectives of those adults who deal with children should be to help them reduce stress by making a change in the environment and/or making a change in the children themselves.

It is well known that each person has a *tolerance level* as far as stress is concerned, and if the stress becomes considerably greater than the tolerance, a person will suffer from emotional stress and its consequent unhappy circumstances.

Indeed, the average child's environment abounds with many stress-inducing factors—society in general, the home, and the school. Factors such as adult behaviors can have a frustrating influence on children. All of these concerns, as well as others, will be addressed in subsequent sections of this chapter.

Not all problems concerned with childhood stress are necessarily evident in the adult population. One such problem is that children are not as likely to be able to cope with stress as successfully as adults can. One prominent child psychologist, Margaret Holland,[1] makes the fol-

---

[1]Holland, Margaret, Report on a proseminar institute in Washington, DC, *The Washington Post*, June 13, 1980.

lowing comparisons between choices in coping with stress open to children and adults.

1. An open display of anger is often considered unacceptable for children. For example, a teacher can be angry with a student, but children may not have the same right to be angry with a teacher.
2. Adults have the latitude of withdrawing or walking out, but this same option of freedom may not be available to children.
3. It is the belief of some child psychologists that *daydreaming* is therapeutic and productive. At the same time, children may be reprimanded for "daydreaming" in school.
4. An adult can get a prescription for "nerves" from a physician — another option not available to children.

As a result, it is likely that children, more often than not, may be punished for using some of the same kinds of stress-coping techniques that are satisfactory for adults. Yet, some of these behaviors are considered socially unacceptable as far as children are concerned.

THE MEANING OF STRESS

There is no solid agreement regarding the derivation of the term *stress*. Some sources suggest that the term is derived from the Latin word *stringere* meaning to "bind tightly." Other sources contend that the term derives from the French word *destress* (English — *distress*) and suggest that the prefix "dis" was eventually eliminated because of slurring, as in the case of the word *because* sometimes becoming '*cause*.

A common generalized literal description of the term is a "constraining force or influence." When applied to human beings, this could be interpreted to mean the extent to which the body can withstand a given force or influence. In this regard one of the most often quoted descriptions of stress is that of the late Hans Selye, who described it as the "nonspecific response of the body to any demand made upon it." (Dr. Selye, one of the most renowned scientists of modern times, has generally been referred to as the "Father of Stress." It was the good fortune of the present authors to collaborate with him on certain aspect of childhood stress; and we prepared a chapter for his third volume of stress research.[2])

Selye's definition means that stress involves a mobilization of the

[2]Humphrey, James H., and Humphrey, Joy N., *Stress in Childhood*, in *Selye's Guide to Stress Research*, Volume 3, Edited by Hans Selye, New York, Van Nostrand Reinhold, 1983, pp. 136–163.

bodily resources in response to some sort of stimulus (stressor). These responses can include various physical and chemical changes in the body. This description of stress could be extended by saying that it involves demands that tax and/or exceed the resources of the human body. This means that stress not only involves these bodily responses, but that it also involves wear and tear on the body brought about by these responses. In essence, stress can be considered as any factor acting internally or externally that makes it difficult to adapt and that induces increased effort on the part of a person to maintain a state of balance within himself and with his external environment. It should be understood that stress is a *state* that one is in, and this should not be confused with any stimuli that produces such a state (stressors).

THE CONCEPT OF STRESS

In discussing the stress concept we do not intend to get into a highly technical discourse on the complex and complicated aspect of stress. Nonetheless, there are certain basic understandings that need to be taken into account, and this requires the use of some technical terms. For this reason we are providing a "minidictionary" of terms used in the discussion to follow.

ACTH—(AdrenoCorticoTropicHormone) secreted by the pituitary gland. It influences the function of the adrenals and other glands in the body.

ADRENALIN—A hormone secreted by the medulla of the adrenal glands.

ADRENALS—Two glands in the upper posterior part of the abdomen that produce and secrete hormones. They have two parts, the outer layer, called the *cortex* and the inner core called the *medulla.*

CORTICOIDS—Hormones produced by the adrenal cortex, an example of which is *cortisone.*

ENDOCRINE—Glands that secrete their hormones into the blood stream.

HORMONE—A chemical produced by a gland, secreted into the blood stream, and influencing the function of cells or organs.

HYPOTHALAMUS—The primary activator of the autonomic nervous system, it plays a central role in translating neurological stimuli into endocrine processes during stress reactions.

PITUITARY—An endocrine gland located at the base of the brain about the size of a pea. It secretes important hormones, one of which is the ACTH hormone.

THYMUS—A ductless gland that is considered a part of the endocrine gland system, located behind the upper part of the breast bone.

Although there are various theories of stress, one of the basic and better known ones is that of the previously-mentioned Hans Selye. We have already given Selye's description of stress as the "nonspecific response of the body to any demand made upon it." The physiological processes and the reactions involved in Selye's stress model is identified as the *General Adaptation Syndrome* and consists of the three stages of *alarm reaction, resistance stage,* and the *exhaustion stage.*

In the first stage (alarm reaction), the body reacts to the stressor and causes the hypothalamus to produce a biochemical "messenger," which in turn causes the pituitary gland to secrete ACTH into the blood. This hormone then causes the adrenal gland to discharge adrenalin and other corticoids. This causes shrinkage of the thymus with an influence on heart rate, blood pressure and the like. It is during the alarm stage that the resistance of the body is reduced.

In the second stage, *resistance* develops if the stressor is not too pronounced. Body adaptation develops to fight back the stress or possibly to avoid it, and the body begins to repair damage, if any.

The third stage of *exhaustion* occurs if there is long-continued exposure to the same stressor. The ability of adaptation is eventually exhausted and the signs of the first stage (alarm reaction) reappear. Selye contended that our adaptation resources are limited, and when they become irreversible, the result is death. (The goal of all of us, of course, should be to keep our resistance and capacity for adaptation.)

Although Selye's stress model which places emphasis upon "nonspecific" responses has been widely accepted, in recent years the nonspecific nature of stress has been questioned by some. Findings of such notable scientists as John Mason of Yale University tend to support the idea that there are other hormones involved in stress in addition to those of the pituitary-adrenal system.

As in the case of all scientific research, the search for truth continues and more sophisticated procedures will emerge in the study of stress. Current theories will be more critically appraised, and other theories will be advanced. In the meantime, there is abundant evidence to support the notion that stress in modern society is a serious threat to the well-being of man if not controlled, and of course, the most important factor in such control is man himself.

HOME STRESS

Changes in society with consequent changes in conditions in some homes are likely to make child adjustment a difficult problem. Such factors as changes in standards of female behavior, larger percentages of both parents working, economic conditions, mass media such as television, as well as numerous others can complicate the life of the modern-day child.

Some child psychiatrists are convinced that some home conditions can have an extremely negative influence on the personality and mental health of some children, not only at their present state of development, but in the future as well. In fact, studies show that the interaction of stress factors is especially important. Most of these studies tend to identify the following factors to be strongly associated with childhood (and possibly later) psychiatric disorders: (1) severe marital discord, (2) low social status, (3) overcrowding or large family size, (4) paternal criminality, (5) maternal psychiatric disorder, and (6) admission into the care of local authorities.

It is estimated that, with only one of the above conditions present, a child is no more likely to develop psychiatric problems than any other child. However, when two of the conditions occur, the child's psychiatric risk increases fourfold.

In our own extensive surveys, we have found that there were certain actions of parents that induced stress in teachers, and according to the teachers, these parental attitudes might well be considered as stress inducing factors for their students.[3]

Actions of parents that induce stress in teachers can be classified into three areas: (1) lack of concern of parents for their children, (2) parental interference, and (3) lack of parental support for teachers.

In almost half of the cases, lack of parental concern for children was stressful for teachers. They cited such things as parents not caring when a student did poorly, parents not willing to help their children with school work, a lack of home discipline, and stress placed on teachers by the difficult time they had getting parents to conferences.

---

[3]Humphrey, James H., and Humphrey, Joy N., Factors which induce stress in teachers, *STRESS*, The Official Journal of the International Institute of Stress, Volume 2, No. 4, Winter 1981.

About a third of the teachers say parental interference was often a result of parents having expectations too high for their children, and this in turn, resulted in parental pressures on children particularly for grades, which may be one of the most serious conditions in schools today—from kindergarten through the university level. In fact, it could be that pressure exerted by parents for grades might be a contributing cause of the increase in the suicide rate among students. Moreover, there are some who believe that parents are literally "driving their children to drink" because of an increase in alcohol consumption, possibly due to the "grade pressure syndrome."

The third classification of parental actions causing stress for teachers is that of lack of parental support, and slightly less than one-fourth have identified stress-inducing factors here. They were stressed by such factors as not being backed by parents and a general poor attitude of parents toward teachers.

Another important home condition that can induce stress in children is when the family itself is under stress. Parenting itself is an extremely difficult task and the demands of this task are becoming more and more complicated. Consequently, many of the pressures that modern parents are called upon to endure cannot only cause stress for them but can also cause them to induce stress upon their children as well.

It has been estimated that one million or more children are abused or neglected by their parents or other "overseers" in our country annually, and that as many as 2,000 die as a result of maltreatment. Authorities suggest that most of this is not caused by inhuman, hateful intent on the part of parents, but rather it is the result of a combination of factors including both the accumulation of stresses on families and unmet needs of parents for support in coping with their child-rearing responsibilities.[4]

SCHOOL STRESS

There are a number of conditions existing in most school situations that can cause much stress for children. These conditions prevail at all levels—possibly in different ways—from the time a child enters school until graduation from college.

---

[4]Johnston, Carol A., *Families in Stress*, Department of Health and Human Services, Washington, DC, HHS Publications No. (OHDS) 80-30162.

Stress and the Child in the Educative Process

School anxiety as a child stressor is a phenomenon with which educators, particularly teachers, frequently find themselves confronted in their dealings with children. Various theories have been advanced to explain this phenomenon and relate it to other character traits and emotional dispositions. Literature on the subject reveals the following characteristics of anxiety as a stress inducing factor in the educative process.

1. Anxiety is considered a learnable reaction that has the properties of a response, a cue of danger, and a drive.
2. Anxiety is internalized fear aroused by the memory of painful past experiences associated with punishment for the gratification of an impulse.
3. Anxiety in the classroom interferes with learning, and whatever can be done to reduce it should serve as a spur to learning.
4. Test anxiety is near-universal experience, especially in this country, which is a test-giving and test-conscious culture.
5. Evidence from clinical studies points clearly and consistently to the disruptive and distracting power of anxiety effects over most kinds of thinking.

It would seem that causes of anxiety change with age as do perceptions of stressful situations. Care should be taken in assessing the total life space of the child—background, home life, school life, age, and sex—in order to minimize the anxiety experienced in the school. It seems obvious that school anxiety, although manifested in the school environment, may often be caused by unrelated factors outside the school.

Conners[5] studied certain interactions with the educative process as they relate to stress. He discussed growing evidence that the designed environment of schools may stress users of the facility both directly and indirectly. Several areas where the designed environment, both on a school-wide and classroom level, interacts with the educational process were explored, and these interactions were considered from the perspective of stresses imposed on teacher and student. Seating position, classroom design and arrangement, density and crowding, privacy, and noise were considered. He suggests that schools need to provide places that will enhance goals of interaction, for participation in social networks,

---

[5]Conners, D. A., The school environment: A link to understanding stress, *Theory into Practice* 22, (1983): 15–20.

and for control over the time and place for social interaction. Relatively minor design modifications introduced into already functioning class-rooms have been shown to produce changes in students' spatial behavior, increased interaction with materials, and decreased interruption.

Obviously, cognitive behaviors are important in the educative process and for success in school. In this regard, Houston, Fox, and Forbes[6] studied this factor as it was concerned with children's state anxiety and performance under stress. They evaluated the relations between trait anxiety in children and state anxiety, cognitive behaviors, and perform-ance in a single study in which two levels of stress were experimentally manipulated.

Sixty-seven fourth-grade children (41 females, 26 males) anticipated and performed a mathematics task in either a high- or a low-stress condition. While the children anticipated performing the task, measures of seven cognitive behaviors were obtained by means of a think-aloud procedure and a cognitive behavior questionnaire. The children were also administered the State-Trait Anxiety for Children. Trait anxiety was found to be related to the state anxiety and the cognitive behaviors of preoccupation and, for females, justification of positive attitudes. The performance of high but not low trait-anxious children was affected by levels of success. This finding aids in reconciling discrepancies in previ-ous research concerning children's trait anxiety and performance.

If the child is to be successful in the educative process, it is imperative that he or she be able to make the best use of native intelligence. The fact that stress can have a negative impact on IQ and task performance is shown in the work of Brown and Rosenbaum,[7] two eminent researchers on the subject. The following discussion consists of some of the excerpted materials of their works in this field.

They examined the effects of stress on IQ in a sample of 4,154 of 41,540 seven-year-old children from the Collaborative Project. They developed a stress index which was a composite score of the number of medical/psychological problems found in a child. The variables were selected from the Collaborative Project data files collected in the 1960s. They included mother's marital status, employment, family configuration, history of illness, death and divorce in the family, measures of auto-

---

[6]Houston, B., Fox, J. E., and Forbes, L., Trait anxiety and children's state anxiety, cognitive behaviors, and performance under stress, *Cognitive Therapy Research* 8 (1984), 631–641.

[7]Brown, Bernard and Rosenbaum, Lilian, Stress and competence, Chap. 7 in *Stress in Childhood*, ed. James H. Humphrey, New York, AMS Press, Inc., 1984, pp. 127–154.

nomic function, achievement measures, and physician-identified health disorders including vision, motor, speech, and hearing problems. They found an inverted-U curve of performance on the WISC IQ test and its component subtest for IQ vs. stress level as measured by total number of problems per child. For example, on the WISC Information subtest, white middle-class children with three problems scored the equivalent of eight IQ points higher than those with no problems and 13 points higher than those with 10 problems. The Information, Block Design, and Coding subtests have the greatest sensitivity to stress, and the Comprehension and Vocabulary subtests were the least sensitive. The inverted-U curve of the full-scale WISC IQ test was less pronounced than the curves of the subtests, with only a seven-point difference between maximum performance level and the performance level under high stress. The curves of low-SES children were of the same inverted-U form but were peaked at lower stress levels, suggesting higher arousal and stressor levels. Thus, the researchers showed that stress has a large effect on intelligence test scores.

On the basis of their work and a review of the literature, they have put forward a body of evidence to support the hypothesis that stress affects intelligence. They presented evidence that many families are exposed to high stressor levels, both acute and chronic. Stress affects the level of anxiety, sense of mastery, self-esteem, depression, and general ability to function in the family which in turn shapes children's competence. Stressors influence performance, both immediately and developmentally, as they interact with genetics, environment, and experience to shape physical, social, emotional, and intellectual development.

They have also presented evidence that acute stressors disrupt the balance between cognitive and emotional function as highly differentiated thought decreases and the brain becomes emotionally overreactive. Children who experience chronic stressors, either real or perceived, show a long-term in decline in intelligence if their coping skills are inadequate, while children with appropriate coping skills rise in intelligence.

They suggest that the hypothesis that stress affects competence implies a different set of interventions in dealing with dysfunction in children and families. Competence in functioning can be altered by modifying the degree of individual differentiation, the intensity, frequency, and predictability of the stressor, and/or the individual's response (arousal) to the stressors and processes of family function. These interpretations can alter the present competence of the individual as well as presumably counter the transmission of suboptimal functioning across generations. These include education in family processes and/or therapy as well as training in a variety of self-regulation techniques such as biofeedback and stress management. There are ways to increase the number of stress-resisting factors to protect children from unnecessary risk. There can be intervention in schools and other organizations to insure that organizational processes do not lead to overreactivity in children and families.

Stress and School Adjustment

One of the most stressful life events for young children is beginning the first grade. One of the reasons for this may possibly be that older childhood friends, siblings, and even some unthinking parents admonish the child with "wait until you get to school—you're going to get it." This kind of negative attitude is likely to increase any "separation anxiety" that the child already has.

As mentioned previously, such separation anxiety begins in the first stage of the child's development, from birth to about 15 months. It can reach a peak in the latter part of the developmental stage from three to five years because it is the first attempt to become a part of the outer world—the school. For many children this is the first task of enforced separation. For those who do not have a well-developed sense of continuity, the separation might be easily equated with the loss of the life-sustaining mother. The stress associated with such a disaster could be overwhelming for such a child. Learning to tolerate the stress of separation is one of the central concerns of preschoolers; adults should be alert to signs and seek to lessen the impact. Compromises should be worked out, not necessarily to remove the stress, but to help the child gradually build a tolerance for separation.

It has been suggested by Chandler[8] that in extreme cases of the separation problem, a child's reaction may typically include temper tantrums, crying, screaming, and downright refusal to go to school. Or, in some cases, suspiciously sudden aches and pains might serve to keep the "sick" child home. What the child is reacting against is not the school but separation from the mother. The stress associated with this event may be seen by the child as a devastating loss equated with being abandoned. The child's behavior in dealing with the stress can be so extreme as to

---

[8]Chandler, L. A., *Children Under Stress*, Springfield, IL, Charles C Thomas, Publisher, 1982, p. 26.

demand special treatment on the part of the significant adults in his or her life.

The aim in such cases should always be to ease the transition into school. It is important to keep in mind that separation is a two-way street. Assuring parents of the competency of the school staff and the physical safety of their child may go a long way toward helping to lessen the stress. If adults act responsibly and with consistence, the child should be able to make an adequate adjustment to this daily separation from family and, in the process, learn an important lesson in meeting reality demands.

Some studies concerning stress and school adjustment have been conducted in recent years and some representative examples of these follows.

Sterling[9] examined the recent stressful life events and young children's school adjustment. A total of 211 first-fourth graders who had experienced one or more stressful life events (SLEs) were compared to a demographically matched sample of 211 children who had not experienced SLEs on measures of school adjustment problems and competencies.

The children's teachers completed the Classroom Adjustment Rating Scale, the Health Resources Inventory, and a 40-item measure of SLEs, background, and personal characteristics for each child. SLEs were found to be associated with the presence of more serious school adjustment problems and fewer competencies. Those associations were strongest for children who had experienced multiple recent SLEs. The importance of preventive interventions for this at-risk group was emphasized.

Stress of young children transferring to new schools was studied by Field.[10] Fourteen preschool children who were transferring to new schools were observed during a two-week period prior to the separation from their 14 classmates who were not transferring. The children ranged in age from 2.9 to 5 years. They were interviewed with the Piers-Harris Children's Self-Concept Scale and the Depression Rating Scale for Children. Parents and teachers completed questionnaires on child behavior. Results showed that children leaving the school, compared to those who were staying, showed increases (compared to baseline observations three months earlier) in fantasy play, physical contact, negative statements and affect, fussiness, activity level, tonic heart rate, and illness as well as

[9]Sterling, S., Recent stressful events and young children's school adjustment. *Journal of Community Psychology* 13, 1985, 87–98.

[10]Field, T., Separation stress for young children transferring to new schools, *Developmental Psychology* 20, 1984, 786–792.

changes in eating and sleeping patterns. Shortly after their departure, this agitated behavior appeared to diminish in the children who were leaving but increased for those who remained in the school. This behavior pattern may represent a coping response to separation in an environment that is laden with cues of losses associated with separation.

In a similar study Blair, Marchant, and Medway[11] considered the problem of aiding the relocated family and mobile child. They were concerned with methods that have proved successful in integrating mobile students into a new school, and they provided an overview of a program developed by them to help highly mobile families deal with moving-related stress.

A summer visitation program was designed to meet the social and emotional needs of entering students by making the family more aware of school policies, developing lines of communication between the family and school, and welcoming the family into the community. The program of Students Assimilated into Learning was designed to aid large numbers of mobile children, with an emphasis on remediation. Other techniques for aiding mobile children included entrance interviews, orientation cycles, and mobility groups. The project of these researchers was directed at parents stationed at a large military base and was designed to sensitize parents about children's feelings about moving and the ways they may express those feelings. Concrete suggestions for helping children with moving were included.

The Stressfulness of Competition in the School Environment

Most of the literature on competition for children has focused on sports activities; however, there are many situations that exist in some classrooms that can cause *competitive stress.* An example is the antiquated "spelling bee" which still exists in some schools and, in fact, continues to be recognized in an annual national competition. Perhaps the first few children "spelled down" are likely to be the ones who need spelling practice the most. And, to say the least, it can be embarrassing in front of others to fail in any school task.

It is interesting to note that the terms *cooperation* and *competition* are antonymous; therefore, the reconciliation of children's competitive needs

---

[11]Blair, J. P., Marchant, K. H., and Medway, F. J., Aiding the relocated family and mobile child, *Elementary School Guidance and Counseling,* 18, 1984, 251–259.

and cooperative needs is not an easy matter. In a sense we are confronted with an ambivalent condition that, if not carefully handled, could place children in a state of conflict, thus causing them to suffer stress.

This was recognized by Horney[12] over a half century ago when she indicated that on the one hand everything is done to spur us toward success, which means that we must not only be assertive but aggressive, able to push others out of the way. On the other hand, we are deeply imbued with ideals which declare that it is selfish to want anything for ourselves, that we should be humble, turn the other cheek, be yielding. Thus, society not only rewards one kind of behavior (cooperation) but its direct opposite (competition) as well. Perhaps more often than not our cultural demands sanction these rewards without provision of clear-cut standards of value with regard to specific conditions under which these forms of behavior might well be practiced. Thus, the child is placed in somewhat of a quandary as to when to compete and when to cooperate.

More recently it has been found that competition does not necessarily lead to peak performance and may in fact interfere with achievement. In this connection Kohn[13] reported on a survey on the effects of competition on sports, business, and classroom achievement and found that 65 studies showed that cooperation promoted higher achievement than competition, eight showed the reverse and 36 showed no statistically significant difference. It was concluded that the trouble with competition is that it makes one person's success depend upon another's failure, and as a result when success depends on sharing resources, competition can get in its way.

In studying about competitive stress Scanland and Passer[14] described this condition as occurring when a child feels (perceives) that he or she will not be able to perform adequately to the performance demands of competition. When the child feels this way, he or she experiences considerable threat to self-esteem which results in stress. They further describe competitive stress as the negative emotion or anxiety that a child experiences when he or she perceives the competition to be personally threatening. Indeed, this is a condition that should not be allowed to prevail in the school environment.

---

[12]Horney, Karen, *The Nerotic Personality of Our Times*, New York, W. W. Norton and Co., Inc., 1937.

[13]Kohn, A., *No Contest: The Case Against Competition*, Boston, Houghton-Mifflin, 1986.

[14]Scanlan, Tara K., and Passer, M. W., *The Psychological and Social Affects of Competition*, Los Angeles, University of California, 1977.

In generalizing on the basis of the available evidence with regard to the subject of competition, the present authors believe that it seems justifiable to formulate the following concepts.

1. Very young children in general are not very competitive but become more so as they grow older.
2. There is a wide variety in competition among children; that is, some are violently competitive, while others are mildly competitive, and still others are not competitive at all.
3. Boys tend to be more competitive than girls.
4. Competition should be adjusted so that there is not a preponderant number of winners over losers.
5. Competition and rivalry produce results in effort and speed of accomplishment.

Certain School Subjects Can Be Stressful

There are various school subject areas that could be considered as perennial nemeses for many students. Probably any subject could be stress inducing for certain students. Prominent among those subjects that have a reputation for being more stress inducing than others are those concerned with the *3Rs.* For example, it has been reported that for many children, attending school daily and performing poorly is a source of considerable and prolonged stress. If the children overreact to environmental stresses in terms of increased muscle tension, they may interfere easily with the fluid muscular movement required in handwriting tasks, decreasing their performance and further increasing environmental stresses. Most educators have seen children squeeze their pencils tightly, press hard on their paper, purse their lips, and tighten their bodies, using an inordinate amount of energy and concentration to write while performing at a very low level.[15]

Reading is another area of school activity that is loaded with anxiety, stress, and frustration for many children. In fact, one of the levels of reading recognized by reading specialists is called the "frustration level." In terms of behavioral observations this can be described as the level in which children evidence tension, excessive or erratic body movements, nervousness and distractibility. This frustration level is said to be a sign

---

[15]Carter, John L. and Russell, Harold L., Relationship between reading frustration and muscle tension in children with reading disabilities, *American Journal of Clinical Feedback*, February 1979, p. 2.

of emotional tension or stress with breakdowns in fluency and a significant increase in reading errors.

A study by Swain[16] was undertaken to determine the extent to which stress was a factor in primary school children's reading difficulties. She investigated referral and evaluation statements and diagnostic data from parents, teachers, reading specialists, and counselors regarding signs of stress and potential stressors as factors in the reading difficulties of 77 primary school children referred for evaluation at the Pupil Appraisal Center (PAC) at North Texas State University between 1977 and 1984.

Situational analysis was employed to obtain a holistic view of each child's reading difficulties. The researcher collected data from documented files at PAC. Data analysis via a categorical coding system produced 39 stress-related categories, organized under broad headings of family and school environment, readiness for reading/learning, general stress reactions, and responses to stress when reading/learning becomes a problem.

The most significant signs of stress cited in this study were symptoms of anxiety and a marked tendency toward passivity and unassertiveness. Primary potential stressors also emerged. Intellectual and language deficits were noted, along with self-defeating behaviors, absence of self-motivating/self-control, and problems stemming from the home and school environment.

Support for findings in referral and evaluation statements was found in diagnostic data which included intelligence, reading and projective tests. Some of the children had specific personal limitations that might have hindered reading. However, many were experiencing frustrations from working at capacity and yet not meeting parental or teacher expectations. No child was found to be coping effectively with apparent adverse circumstances. Failure by many of these children to adapt successfully to stress in their personal lives could forecast chronic difficulty in reading when it, too, becomes a challenge for them.

The subject that appears to stress the greatest majority of students is mathematics. This condition prevails from the study of arithmetic upon entering school through the required courses in mathematics in college. This has become such a problem in recent years that there is now an area of study called "math anxiety" that is receiving increasing attention.

---

[16]Swain, C. J., Stress as a factor in primary school children's reading problems, *Doctoral Dissertation*, North Texas State University, Denton, TX, 1985.

Prominent among those studying this phenomenon is Sheila Tobias,[17] some of whose findings are summarized in the following discussion.

There appears to be what could be called "math anxious" and "math avoiding" people who tend not to trust their problem-solving abilities and who experience a high level of stress when asked to use them. Even though these people are not necessarily "mathematical ignorant," they tend to feel that they are, simply because they cannot focus on the problem at hand or because they are unable to remember the appropriate formula. Thus, a feeling of frustration and incompetence are likely to make them reluctant to deal with mathematics in their daily lives. It is suggested that at the root of this self-doubt is a fear of making mistakes and appearing stupid in front of others.

It is believed that there are at least three sources of anxiety commonly found in traditional mathematics classes: (1) time pressure, (2) humiliation, and (3) emphasis on one right answer.

As far as time pressure is concerned, such things as flash cards, timed tests, and competition in which the object is to finish first are among the first experiences that can make lasting negative impressions, and slower learners are soon likely to become apprehensive when asked to perform a mathematics problem.

One of the strongest memories of some math-anxious adults is the feeling of humiliation when being called upon to perform in front of the class. The child may be asked to go to the chalkboard to struggle over a problem until a solution is found. If an error is made, the child may be prodded to locate and correct it. In this kind of stressful situation it is not surprising that the child is likely to experience "math block," which adds to his sense of humiliation and failure. This should not be interpreted to mean that the chalkboard should not be used creatively to demonstrate problem-solving abilities. A child who successfully performs a mathematical task in front of classmates can have the enjoyable experience of instructing others. Also, the rest of the class can gain useful information from watching how another solves a problem. When using chalkboard practice, however, it is important to remember that children profit from demonstrating their competence and not their weaknesses.

Although mathematics problems do, in most cases, have right answers, it can be a mistake to always focus attention on accuracy. In putting too much emphasis on the end product, oftentimes overlooked is the valu-

---

[17]Tobias, Sheila, Stress in the math classroom, *Learning*, January 1981.

able information about the process involved in arriving at that product. It would be well for teachers to reward creative thinking as well as correct answers. Again, the reader should not interpret this as meaning that the right answer is not important. However, when it is emphasized to the exclusion of all other information, students can become fearful of making mistakes and possibly angry with themselves when they do.

Test Anxiety

Two prominent authorities on the subject, Bernard Brown and Lilian Rosenbaum[18] contend that perceived stress appears to depend on psychological sets and responses that individuals are more likely to bring into the testing situation than manufacture on the spot. Students respond to tests and testing situations with learned patterns of stress reactivity. The patterns may vary among individuals and may reflect differences in autonomic nervous system conditioning, feelings of threat or worry regarding the symbolic meaning of the test or the testing situation, and coping skills that govern the management of complexity, frustration, information load, symbolic manipulation, and mobilization of resources. There are also individual patterns of maladaptive behavior such as anxiety, a sustained level of autonomic activity after exposure to a stressor and the use of a variety of such defense mechanisms as learned helplessness and avoidance behavior.

Perceived stress also depends upon the nature of the task to be performed. As tasks get more complex and require greater degrees of coordination and integration of the nervous system, a given stressor level will affect task performance as if it were a stronger stressor.

What then does the nature of test anxiety imply for educational goals and practices? Perhaps there should be a continuing opportunity for all school personnel and parents to report on their experiences with the tests that have been used. This feedback should also place a great deal of emphasis on the students' reactions to their testing experience. It is essential that the reactions of children that give evidence to emotional disturbance in relation to tests be carefully considered, especially when test results are interpreted and used for instructional guidance and administrative purposes.

---

[18]Brown, Bernard and Rosenbaum, Lilian, Stress and competence, Chapter 7 in *Stress in Childhood*, edited by James H. Humphrey, New York, AMS Press, Inc., 1984 pp. 127–154.

Adults, particularly parents and teachers, can be of assistance to children in the rigors of test-taking. Various recommendations have been made with reference as to how this can be accomplished. One qualified expert, Barbara Kuczen,[19] Professor of Early Childhood Education at Chicago State University, believes that the following suggestions can relieve pressure from the testing scene.

1. Explain the purpose of tests, and make it clear that the child's best is expected, but no more. In this way the child can prepare and relax going into the test, knowing that maximum effort is being expended.

2. When it is known that a test is scheduled, the child should get a good night's sleep, eat a well-balanced breakfast, be dressed in comfortable clothes and leave home in a relaxed unrushed state.

3. When a test paper is returned, immediately go over the answers and analyze errors. Clear up any misunderstandings about directions, terms or answers so the child will be better prepared next time.

4. Give the child experience working under rigid time limits. Play some games in which the child is timed or allowed a designated number of minutes for completing a task.

5. Advise the child not to get "hung up" on a difficult question, but instead to skip it and do it later, if there is time.

6. Have the child learn to pace the work by looking over the material to see how much needs to be done.

7. Have the child practice reading a question in one place and recording the answer on a separate sheet of paper.

8. Adults should not magnify the importance of tests by getting overexcited by good, or poor, scores. Let the child know that the learning that occurs in school is the prime concern. Test results should reflect that learning.

9. Help the child understand that some test stress can motivate a student to study and achieve. However, if stress is extreme, it can cripple the learner. Work on using ways to relax.

10. Help the child understand that test stress caused by not studying is likely to be inevitable and unacceptable.

Finally, it is important to take a positive attitude when considering test results. That is, emphasis should be placed on the number of answers

---

[19]Kuczen, Barbara, *Childhood Stress Don't Let Your Child be a Victim*, New York, Delacorte Press, 1982, p. 194–195.

that were correct. For example, the child will more likely be encouraged if you say, "You got seven right," rather than "You missed three." It has been our experience that this approach can help minimize stress in future test-taking.

Is the School Learning Environment More Stressful for Boys than for Girls?

In general, emotional stress seems to have a greater effect on boys than on girls in both the school and home environments. One possible exception to this in the school situation is that girls are prone to suffer more anxiety over report cards than are boys. Most studies show that boys are much more likely to be stressed by family discord and disruption than are girls, although there does not seem to be a completely satisfactory explanation for this.

In any event, it is interesting to note that many people have been critical of the early school learning environment particularly as far as boys are concerned. Some of these critics have gone so far as to say that young boys are being discriminated against in their early school years. Let us examine the premise.

A generally accepted description of the term *learning* is that it involves some sort of change in behavior. Many learning theorists maintain that behavior is a product of heredity and environment. Unquestionably, it is very apparent that environment plays a major role in determining one's behavior, and some tend to feel that man is, indeed, controlled by his environment. Nevertheless, we must remember that it is an environment largely of his own making. The issue here is whether or not an environment is provided that is best suited for boys at the early age levels, and further whether such an environment is likely to cause more stress among young boys than young girls.

While the school has no control over ancestry, it can, within certain limitations, exercise some degree of control over the kind of environment in which the learner must function. Generally speaking, it is doubtful that all schools have provided an environment that is most conducive to learning as far as young boys are concerned. Many child development specialists have characterized the environment at the primary level of education as *feminized.*

A major factor to consider is that which concerns the biological differences between boys and girls in this particular age range, and it may be questionable whether educational planning has always taken these important differences into account. Over the years there has been an accumulation of evidence on this general subject appearing in the literature on child development, some of which will be summarized here.

Due to certain hormonal conditions, boys tend to be more aggressive, restless, and impatient. In addition, the male has more rugged bone structure, and as a consequence greater strength than the female at all ages. Because of this, males tend to display greater muscular reactivity that in turn expresses itself in a stronger tendency toward restlessness and vigorous overt activity. This condition is concerned with the greater oxygen consumption required to fulfill the male's need for increased energy production. The male organism might be compared to an engine that operates at higher levels of speed and intensity than the less energetic female organism.

Another factor to take into account is the difference in Basal Metabolic Rate (BMR) in young boys and young girls. The BMR is indicative of the speed at which body fuel is changed into energy, as well as how fast this energy is used. The BMR can be measured in terms of calories per meter of body surface with a calorie representing a unit measure of heat energy in food. It has been found, on average, BMR rises from birth to about three years of age and then starts to decline until the ages of approximately 20 to 24. The BMR is higher for boys than for girls, particularly at the early age levels. Because of the higher BMR, boys in turn will have a higher amount of energy to expend. Because of differences in sex hormonal conditions and BMR, it appears logical to assume that these factors will influence the male in his behavior patterns.

From a growth and development point of view, while at birth the female is from one-half to one centimeter less in length than the male and around 300 grams less in weight, she is perhaps actually a much better developed organism. It is estimated on the average that at the time of entrance into school, the female is usually six to twelve months more physically mature than the male. As a result, girls may be likely to learn earlier how to perform tasks of manual dexterity such as buttoning their clothing. In one of our observational studies of preschool children, we found that little girls were able to perform the task of tying their shoe laces at a rate of almost four times that of little boys.

Although all schools should not be categorized in the same manner, some of them have been captured by the dead hand of tradition and ordinarily provide an environment that places emphasis upon such factors as neatness, orderliness, and passiveness which are easier for girls to conform to than boys. Of course, this may be partly because our culture has tended to force females to be identified with many of these characteristics.

The authoritarian and sedentary classroom atmosphere that prevails in some schools that involves the "sit still and listen" syndrome, fails to take into account the greater activity drive and physical aggressiveness of boys. What have been characterized as feminization traits prevailing in some elementary schools tend to have an adverse influence on the young male child as far as learning is concerned.

Some studies have shown that as far as hyperactivity is concerned, boys may outnumber girls by a ratio of as much as nine to one. This may be one of the reasons why teachers generally tend to rate young males as being so much more aggressive than females, with the result that young boys are considered to be more negative and extroverted. Because of these characteristics, boys generally have poorer relationships with their teachers than do girls, and in the area of behavior problems and discipline in the age range from five to eight years, boys account for twice as many disturbances as girls. The importance of this factor is borne out when it is considered that good teacher-pupil relationships tend to raise the achievement levels of both sexes.

Various studies have shown that girls generally receive higher grades than boys although boys may achieve as well as, and in some instances, better than girls. It is also clearly evident that boys in the early years fail twice as often as girls even when there is no significant difference between intelligence and achievement test scores of both sexes. This suggests that even though both sexes have the same intellectual tools, there are other factors that militate against learning as far as boys are concerned.

If one is willing to accept the research findings and observational evidence appearing in the child development literature regarding the premise outlined here, the question is: What attempts, if any, are being made to improve the condition? At one time it was thought that the solution might lie in defeminization of the schools at the early age levels by putting more men into classrooms. This apparently has met with little success because the learning environment remains essentially the same regardless of the sex of the teacher. Some educators have suggested that little boys start school later or that little girls start earlier. The problem with this, of course, is that state laws concerned with school entrance are likely to distinguish only in terms of age and not gender. In a few remote instances some schools have experimented with separating boys and girls at the early grade levels. In some cases this form of grouping has resulted in both groups achieving at a higher level than when the sexes were in classes together.

The major question that must be posed is: What can be done to at least partially restructure an environment that will be more favorable to the learning of young boys? One step in this direction, recommended by various child development specialists, it to develop curriculum content that is more *action*-oriented, thus taking into account the basic need for motor activity involved in human learning. This is to say that deep consideration might well be given to learning activities through which excess energy, especially of boys, can be utilized. The extent to which this kind of curriculum content would make learning less stressful for boys is not entirely known; however, experimentation by the present authors shows definite possibilities along these lines. (NOTE: For a detailed account of this approach the reader is referred to: Humphrey, James H. and Humphrey, Joy N., *Help Your Child Learn the 3R's Through Activy Play,* Charles C Thomas, 1980.)

Several causes and contributing cause of stress have been dealt with in the preceding discussions. It is possible to eliminate many of these stress-inducing factors. For those that cannot be eliminated entirely, serious attempts should be made to at least keep them under control if we are to succeed in providing for total development of children.

Chapter 8

HEALTH AS A FACTOR IN CHILD DEVELOPMENT

It should be a foregone conclusion that the health of a child is one of the most important factors in his or her development. Yet, when one looks at the comparatively low expenditures for important life values such as education and health, it becomes luminously clear that our national priorities could be subject to question as far as the welfare of the citizenry is concerned. Many critics agree that when a nation spends 15 times as much on the military as it does on education, there appears to be a serious distortion in the allocation of funds.

There are many deficiencies in health care in the so-called "land of plenty." Approximately 37 million Americans have no health insurance; one-third of these are children and teenagers and most of the rest are the working poor. Also this nation's infant mortality rate is among the developed world's highest.[1] And add to this the fact that thousands upon thousands of children are member of families well below the poverty line. This number is increasing tremendously and, according to some experts, is getting out of control.

Consider also the children of the *medical underclass.* Homeless pregnant women are more likely to have higher infant mortality rates than are women living in housing projects. Homeless children are at special risk of malnutrition, anemia, and asthma as well as such illnesses as diptheria, tetanus, measles, and polio. They also suffer a higher rate of emotional and learning problems than the general population.[2]

There is no question about it. A lack of concern for optimum health of children can impact seriously on child development. It is the intent of this final chapter to take into account various aspects of health that are concerned with the development of the child.

---

[1]Cohn, Victor, The disgrace of American health care, *Weekly Journal of Medicine, Science and Society,* January 24, 1989.

[2]Trafford, Abigail, The Reagan legacy—A swelling medical underclass in the land of plenty, *Weekly Journal of Medicine, Science and Society,* January 24, 1989.

THE MEANING OF HEALTH AND RELATED TERMS

The precise meaning that one associates with the term *health* depends in a large measure upon the particular frame of reference in which it is used. In past years, it was a relatively common practice to think of health in terms of the condition of the living organism that functioned normally. This idea about health is one that is still accepted by many people. In subscribing to this particular concept, these individuals tend to think of health predominantly as a state in which there is absence of pain or symptoms related to a poorly functioning organism. When thought of only in this manner, health is considered primarily in terms of a state in which there is absence of disease.

In more recent times, health is being considered more and more in terms of *well-being,* which is perhaps our most important human value. In considering health from a point of view of well-being, the ideal state of health would be one in which all of the various parts of the human organism function at an optimum level at all times. Although it very unlikely that the human organism will ever achieve the ideal state suggested here, such a level is ordinarily used as a standard for diagnosing or appraising the human health status.

The old meaning of health that considered it primarily only in terms of absence of disease tended to place it in a negative sense. The more modern concept places positive emphasis on the term. This is to say that the meaning of health is interpreted as a level of well-being as well. It seems logical to assume that modern society's goal should be directed toward achieving the highest level of well-being for all its citizens.

In view of the above discussion, it is interesting to note the results of our own health surveys of 9- and 10-year-old children. When asked what the word health meant, 70 percent answered that it was concerned with the condition of the body (Examples: when your body is in good condition and to be in good shape). Twenty percent identified health specifically with eating the right foods (Example: when you eat the proper foods). And, ten percent identified health specifically with exercise (Example: when you get lots of exercise).

Health Knowledge, Attitudes and Practice

Any discussion of the meaning of health should consider the three important aspects of health knowledge, health attitudes, and health practice. Each of these dimensions will be dealt with separately, but it appears important at the outset to consider them together for the purpose of a better understanding of how they are related.

In order to benefit most from health learning experiences, it is most important that these experiences develop into desirable health practices. Thus, the ultimate goal should be in the direction of a kind of behavior that will be likely to insure optimum present and future health for the individual. However, before the most desirable and worthwhile health practices can be achieved, there is a need for a certain amount of desirable health knowledge, along with a proper attitude, in making appropriate application of the knowledge to health practice.

Although it is obvious that *to know* is not necessarily *to do*, nevertheless, that which is done wisely will depend in a large measure upon the kind and amount of health knowledge one has acquired. In accumulation of health knowledge, one will need to understand *why* it is beneficial to follow a certain practice. When one knows why, it is perhaps more likely that a desirable *attitude* toward certain health practices will be developed. If a person has a sufficient amount of desirable health knowledge developed through valid health concepts, and also a proper attitude he or she will be more apt to apply the knowledge in health behavior. Moreover, one should be in a better position to exercise good judgment and make wise decisions in matters pertaining to health if the right kind and amount of health knowledge has been obtained.

Health Knowledge

Knowledge about health is acquired in a variety of different ways. Some of it is the product of tradition and, as such, oftentimes is nothing more than folklore. Certain popular notions about health-related matters that have long since been dispelled by the scientific community are still held by many people who have not, for some reason or other, benefited from modern health knowledge.

Other kinds of health knowledge of sorts are derived in our modern society through mass communication media, such as television and radio. Although some of this information may be valid from a health point of view, we should be alert to the possibility that the primary purpose of many kinds of advertising is to sell a product that proclaims results that are not always likely to be attainable.

Another source of health knowledge is the home. In fact, most of our important health learnings get their start in the home. Parents are our first teachers and, for better or for worse, what we learn from them, mostly without our being aware that we are learning it, tends to remain with us. A good home should contribute much to the health knowledge of its children simply by providing good meals and a friendly, well-regulated, but pleasant and recreationally-challenging environment in which to grow. Children from such homes ordinarily do not have to *unlearn* a lot of faulty ideas and unwholesome attitudes when they are in the next great potential source of health knowledge—the schools. It should be borne in mind that many children who grow up in homes in the inner city and some remote parts of the country do not benefit from good home experiences, and thus, their first source of health knowledge is the school.

The scope of knowledge that one might obtain about matters related to health is almost endless, and, obviously, it would be impossible to learn all there is to know about it. However, there are certain basic concepts about health that should be developed by individuals at all age levels. Generally speaking, the individual should acquire knowledge pertaining to the direct basic needs of the human organism, and, in addition, knowledge regarding the organism as it functions in its environment.

A question often raised is: At how early an age level is a child capable of acquiring health knowledge? A recent study by Gary D. Nelson of the Centers for Disease Control in Atlanta, Georgia showed that when children were presented with health knowledge learning experiences at the preschool level, their health knowledge increased.[3]

This study examined the effects of the "Hale and Hardy's Helpful Health Hints" preschool health education curriculum on the health knowledge of children three to five years of age residing in the State of Alabama. The data producing sample in the study consisted of nine experimental preschool programs (194 children) and three comparison group programs (73 children). A picture identification test was used to assess a child's pretest and posttest health knowledge of curriculum content including the five senses, safety, nutrition, dental health, personal responsibility, emotions, hygiene, and drugs/medicines. Inservice training of preschool program teachers and curriculum implementation was completed between the months of October, 1986 and April, 1987.

---

[3]Nelson, Gary D., Effects of a preschool health education curriculum on children's health knowledge, Research Abstracts, American Association for Health, Physical Education, Recreation and Dance, Reston, VA, 1988.

Posttest knowledge scores increased by 22 percent among experimental group preschool programs and 12 percent among comparison group preschool programs. Significant differences between pretest and posttest scores were found within the experimental and comparison group preschool programs. Significant posttest differences between experimental and comparison subjects were found with the individual as the unit of analysis. Test item analysis further indicated specific content strength of the curriculum. Statistical and visual analysis of the results indicate the curriculum had a moderate impact on child health knowledge. The findings of this study highlight issues related to preschool program evaluation including naturalistic versus controlled experimental studies, student versus program as the unit of analysis, and norm referenced versus criterion referenced testing. The findings also provide direction in research efforts which attempt to define the conditions in which preschool health education is most effective.

Health Attitudes

Any discussion of attitudes requires an identification of the meaning of the term. Although it is recognized that different people will attach different meanings to the term attitude, for purposes here we would like to think of attitude as being associated with *feelings.* We hear such expressions as: "How do you *feel* about it?" In a sense, this implies, "What is your *attitude* toward it?" Therefore, theoretically, at least, attitude could be considered a factor in the determination of action because of this feeling about something. For example, knowledge alone that physical exercise is beneficial will not necessarily lead to regular exercising, but a strong feeling or attitude might be a determining factor that leads one to exercise regularly.

It should be mentioned at this point that, contrary to abundant empirical thought, there is little objective evidence to support unequivocally the contention that attitude has a positive direct influence on behavior. One of the difficulties in studying this phenomenon scientifically lies in the questionable validity of instruments used to measure attitudes. Moreover, there is little consistent agreement with regard to the meaning of attitudes. Thus, the position taken here is one of theorectical postulation based upon logical assumption.

As far as health attitudes are concerned, they could well be considered a gap that can possibly exist between health knowledge and health practice, and this gap needs to be bridged if effective health behavior is to result from acquiring valid health knowledge. Let us consider, as an example, a person who has acquired some knowledge regarding the degree to which cigarette smoking can be harmful to health. Perhaps this person will have some sort of underlying feeling toward such knowledge. He or she may choose to disregard it because friends have assumed such an attitude toward it. Or, it may be felt that the evidence is convincing enough to believe that cigarette smoking is something he or she can get along without. In either case, an attitude has been developed toward the practice of cigarette smoking, and it is likely that one may react in accordance with this feeling. It should also be mentioned that one may not necessarily react in accordance with true feelings because it may be considered fashionable to smoke cigarettes so as not to lose status with friends who do. (This is a strong possibility as far as some children are concerned.) Whatever way one chooses to react will be tempered at least to an extent by the consequences associated with the knowledge acquired about cigarette smoking.

Obviously, it would be hoped that the accumulation of health knowledge would be accompanied by a positive attitude, and that this attitude would result in desirable action. It is possible that only in terms of such a positive attitude are desirable health practices, and thus, a better way of living likely to result.

Health Practice

It is a well-known fact that all people do not capitalize on the knowledge they have acquired. Perhaps many are apt to act only on impulse; actions of others are influenced to an extent by their friends. However, in a matter as important as one's health, it appears that a reasonable course to follow would be one in which the individual weighs the facts and scientific evidence before acting.

Perhaps we might look at health practices that are desirable and those that are undesirable, or, in other words, those health practices that will result in pleasantness or unpleasantness. If we weigh knowledge in these terms, perhaps we can appreciate better the possible consequence of certain health practices.

Altering behavior is not always an easy matter; however, it is hoped that most persons will want to make a positive modification of their own health behavior after acquiring desirable health knowledge and forming favorable attitudes. In the final analysis, the individual will make the decisions regarding his or her own health practices. In young children, perhaps these health practices can be forced, although this notion is impractical if we are to expect the best learning to take place; and forcing health practices upon children as they grow older not only appears impractical, but in many cases, unwarranted as well. It is likely this same philosophy can be applied to adults.

As far as personal health is concerned, it perhaps becomes a matter of how much risk one is willing to take, and health practices are likely to be based on this factor. By way of illustration we will refer again to cigarette smoking and health. To our knowledge, it has never been demonstrated scientifically that cigarette smoking is in any way beneficial to the physical health of the human organism; on the contrary, there has been a great deal of information accepted as evidence from a medical point of view that indicates that smoking can contribute to certain types of serious diseases. Yet, untold numbers of individuals are willing to assume a dangerous risk in defiance of such evidence. After a person has learned about some aspect of health, he or she is left with an element of choice. It is hoped that a course of health action would be chosen that would involve a minimum of risk.

In our studies of 9- to 10-year-old children, we asked them to identify what they considered were *good* and *bad* health practices. An overwhelming 86 percent said eating proper foods was a good health practice, and foods most frequently mentioned were milk and fruits and vegetables. Ten percent said "taking the right medicine" was a good health practice, 2 percent said "wearing warm clothes," and the other 2 percent said "taking exercise."

As far as bad health practices are concerned, 55 percent said eating improper foods, some of which were candy, sugar, fats, and the broad classification of "junk foods." (Interestingly enough, we shall see later that the latter is very popular, at least among those in the 10 to 11 year age range). The remaining 45 percent felt that the worst health practice was substance abuse and cited such things as drugs, smoking, and drinking.

THE HEALTH TRIANGLE

Basic to satisfactory child development is the attention significant others in the child's life (and at certain age levels, children themselves) pay to personal health. In discussing the subject of caring for health we like to deal with what we call the "health triangle:" (1) nutrition and diet, (2) physical activity and exercise, and (3) rest and sleep.

Nutrition and Diet

It should be obvious that the areas of nutrition and diet are highly interrelated and interdependent. However, there are certain differences that need to be taken into account, particularly as far as the meaning of these two areas are concerned.

Nutrition

Nutrition can be described as the sum of the processes by which a person takes in and utilizes food substances; that is, the nourishment of the body by food. These processes consist of ingestion, digestion, absorption, and assimilation.

Ingestion derives from the Latin word "ingestus," meaning to take in, and in this context, it means taking in food, or the act of eating. The process of *digestion* involves the breaking down and conversion of food into substances that can be *absorbed* through the lining of the intestinal tract and into the blood and used by the body. *Assimilation* is concerned with the incorporation or conversion of nutrients into *protoplasm,* which is the essential material making up living cells.

The body needs many essential nutrients or foods to keep it functioning properly. These nutrients fall into the broad groups of proteins, carbohydrates, fats, vitamins, and minerals. Although water is not a nutrient in the strictest sense of the word, it must be included, for nutrition cannot take place without it.

Three major functions of nutrients are building and repair of all body tissues, regulation of all body functions, and providing fuel for the body's energy needs. Although all of the nutrients can do their best work when they are in combination with other nutrients, each still has its own vital role to play.

Digestion. The digestive system of the body is more than 30 feet long from beginning to end, and the chemical processes that occur within the walls of this mucus-lined hollow tube are extremely complex in nature. From the moment that food is taken into the mouth until waste products are excreted, the body's chemical laboratory is at work. The principal parts of this system are the alimentary canal, consisting of the oral cavity, pharnyx, esophagus, stomach, small intestine, and large intestine. Two additional organs are necessary to complete the digestive system. These are the liver and the pancreas, both of which connect to the small intestine. It is from these two organs that many of the essential digestive juices are secreted.

As mentioned previously, the function of the digestive system is to change the composition of foods which we ingest. Reduced to simpler chemical substances, the food can be readily absorbed through the lining of the intestines for distribution by the circulatory system to the millions of body cells. These end products of digestion are in the form of simple sugars, fatty acids, amino acids, minerals, and vitamins.

Digestion is also accomplished by mechanical action. First, the food is broken down by the grinding action of the teeth. This increases tremendously the food surface area upon which the various digestive juices can act. It is then swallowed and eventually is moved through the alimentary canal by a process called peristalsis. This is a series of muscular contractions, which mix the contents of the digestive tract and keep it on the move.

The digestive tract is exceedingly responsive to one's emotional state. Food eaten under happy conditions tends to be readily digested. On the contrary, digestion may be impeded and even stopped for a considerable period of time (as much as a day or more) if severe emotional stress occurs. Extensive nerve connections in the digestive tract tend to make its organs especially susceptible to disorders caused by emotional disturbance. Examples of some of these disorders are nausea, diarrhea, and colitis (inflamation of the large bowel). In such disorders the organs involved may not necessarily be diseased and there may only be an impaired functioning of the organ. However, many authorities agree that prolonged emotional stress can lead to serious diseases of the digestive tract.

There is a popular belief that a bowel movement per day is essential to health. Moreover, so common rumor has it, to be really effective, this movement should occur at a particular time each day. "Autointoxication" or self-poisoning, it is sometimes claimed, may otherwise result. As a matter of fact, many people do find a bowel movement once a day satisfactory and having it at a particular time, convenient. However, just as some require more than one elimination per day, others find every other day a natural rhythm—and not a cause of constipation (difficult bowel evacuation—a condition that has Americans spending about a half billion dollars annually on laxatives). Thus, the problem is not one of conforming to an arbitrary standard, but discovering one's own natural rhythm and responding to the urge when it comes.

Various things commonly interrupt individual rhythm. For example, altering one's customary routine, rising at a different hour, failing to exercise, and failing to eat enough food containing roughage which normally stimulates peristaltic action. The resulting feeling of discomfort, headache, or irritability—"constipation symptoms"—do not necessarily result from self-poisoning or autointoxication caused by fecal matter reentering the blood stream. It seems likely that the emphasis that many parents put on "moving the bowels" leads many people to overexaggerate the importance of failing to do so on schedule. Generally speaking, we are inclined to believe that the individual who has a good diet, including adequate fluids, and is active can trust his or her body in this as in other regards to tend to itself in its automatic function. Presupposing a generally healthful pattern of living, perhaps patience rather than grim concern and laxatives is the reasonable prescription. Needless to say, a physician should be consulted in the event of marked or prolonged deviation from one's normal bowel-moving behavior.

Diet

The term *diet* is an all inclusive one used to refer to foods and liquids regularly consumed. The question often raised is: What constitutes a balanced diet? This means essentially, that along with sufficient fluids, one should include foods from the *four basic food groups.* These are the dairy group, the meat group, the vegetable and fruit group, and the bread and cereal group.

A guide to a balanced diet was prepared by the staff of the United States Senate Select Committee on Nutrition and Human Needs. This Committee spent a great deal of time on hearings and research, and some of its recommendations are listed as follows.

1. Eat less meat and more fish and poultry.
2. Replace whole milk with skim milk.
3. Reduce intake of eggs, butter, and other high-cholesterol sources.
4. Cut back on sugars to 15 percent of daily caloric intake.
5. Reduce intake of salt to a total of three grams a day.
6. Eat more fruit, vegetables, and whole grain.

The above recommendations are directed to the general population. However, one important factor must be recommended, and this is that eating is an individual matter. The problem may not be so much one of following an arbitrary diet, but one of learning to know on what foods and proportions of foods one functions best. The body is capable of compensating for an imbalance in nutrients that we fail to get if the shortage is made up within a reasonable period of time. In other words, it is not necessary to have an exactly balanced diet at every meal. Indeed, it is possible to miss meals—even go for several days without food—and show no signs of malnutrition. The important consideration seems to be in the quality of the total intake over periods of time.

The foregoing observations should not be interpreted to mean that one should be indifferent or careless about food choices. After all, you quite literally are what you eat. It is absurd that some people are more careful about what they feed their pets than they are about what they feed themselves. This kind of thoughtlessness has given rise to the claim that Americans are the most overfed and malnourished people in the world. (Any radical depature from one's diet should be made only under the guidance of a physician and/or a qualified nutritionist.)

Eating Habits of Children

Adult supervision, especially that of parents, is of utmost importance in children's eating habits. However, unfortunately in some cases some parents may be the child's worst enemy as far as eating habits are concerned. The nagging parent who tries to ply the child with foods that he may not like and the constant admonishment of "clean your plate" oftentimes can do a great deal of harm to the child's present and future eating habits.

The diets of some families include too much of certain foods that can be potentially harmful to the adult members as well of its children. A case in point is the intake of *cholesterol.* Excessive amounts of this chemical component of animal oils and fats are deposited in blood vessels and may be a factor in the causation of hardening of the arteries leading to a heart attack.

In his interesting book, *The Healing Heart,* Norman Cousins[4] suggests that the accumulation of these fatty substances is not something that begins in upper middle age. On the contrary, the process can begin in early childhood. A 1982–83 study of children in New York City and Los Angeles conducted by Dr. Ernst L. Wynder of the American Heart Foundation, showed average cholesterol levels of 180 for children in the 10–12 year age range. Continuing at the same course would lead

---

[4]Cousins, Norman, *The Healing Heart,* New York, W. W. Norton & Company, 1983, p. 66.

to cholesterol levels close to or above 300 by the age 35. Physicians vary widely in their beliefs about safe levels of cholesterol and not long ago a very broad range of 150–300 was considered normal. However, recently thoughts on this matter have changed radically. For example, the National Heart, Lung and Blood Institute has announced more stringent guidelines. That is, it is now believed that total blood cholesterol should not go over 200 (this means 200 milligrams of total cholesterol per deciliter of blood).

At about the end of the first year of life children begin to have a rather remarkable change in their eating habits. For one thing, there is likely to be a large decrease in the intake of food. Many parents who do not understand the process of child growth and development worry needlessly about this condition. What actually happens is that after the first year the growth rate of the child declines and as a consequence his need for calories per pound of body weight becomes less. This causes his appetite to decrease and this can vary from one meal to another, sometimes depending upon the kind and amount of activity in which the child engages. Thus, a parent who is aware of this will not expect the child of two or three years of age to eat the way he did when he was six-months old. This knowledge for the parent is very important because then he or she will not be so concerned with the *quantity* of the child's intake of food. This is to say that parents should be more concerned with *quality* of food than amount of intake.

Sometimes a child may develop a sudden like or dislike for certain foods. Reasons vary for this change in attitude. He may want a particular cereal because of a prize in the box, and then he may turn the food down because he is disenchanted and does not want the prize. Fortunately, more often than not, such likes and dislikes are not long-lasting, and adults should not worry too much about them.

It is a good practice to provide a rather large variety of foods early in the child's life. This helps to prevent a child from forming set opinions on food likes and dislikes. Adults should set an example by not allowing their own dislikes to influence children.

Adults often complain that a particular child is a "poor eater." When this occurs it is important to try to identify the cause of this problem. It may be that the child too frequently eats alone, and is deprived of the pleasant company of others. Or perhaps the portions are too large, particularly if he feels that he must consume all of it. As mentioned elsewhere, mealtime should be a happy time. It is not a time for reprimanding and threatening if a child does not eat heartily. Such behavior on the part of adults can place the child under stress and create an eating problem that otherwise would probably not occur.

In our studies of 9–10-year-old children we found that generally those in this age range were aware of foods that were *best* for health and those that were *worst* for health. Those foods identified as "best" were: vegetables, 36 percent; fruits, 28 percent; meat, 26 percent; bread, 8 percent; and somewhat surprisingly, milk only 2 percent. As for the "worst" foods for health: 65 percent said candy and other sweets; 17 percent said junk foods; 9 percent said salt; 5 percent said coffee; and 4 percent said fats.

In one interesting study[5] children in the 10–11 year age range were asked to name their favorite foods. The results in order of preference: pizza, hamburgers, spaghetti, ice cream, hot dogs, popcorn, and brownies. Of course, these results should not be misterpreted to suggest that these foods consist of a child's regular diet, but rather they are the foods they tend to like best. Nonetheless, a disturbing estimate is that Americans take as many as one-half of their meals out—and that these out-of-home meals are likely to be taken at the "fast food" establishments.

Physical Activity and Exercise

When used in connection with the human organism, the term "physical" means a concern for the body and its needs. The term "activity" derives from the word "active," one meaning of which is the requirement of action. Thus, when the two words physical and activity are used together, it implies body action. This is a broad term and could include any voluntary and/or involuntary body movement. When such body movement is practiced for the purpose of developing and maintaining physical fitness, it is ordinarily referred to as physical exercise.

Physical Activity for Children

One of the most important characteristics of life is movement. Whatever else they may involve, practically all of our achievements are based on our ability to move. Obviously, the very young child is not a highly intelligent being in the sense of abstract thinking, and he only gradually acquires the ability to deal with symbols and intellectualize his experience in the course of his development. Any effort to help the child grow,

---

[5]Mini Page, *The Washington Post*, December 25, 1988.

develop, learn, and be reasonably free from stress and tension must take this dominance of movement in the life of the child into account.

Practically all children—unless there is an incapitating impairment—will engage in physical activity if given the opportunity to do so. They run, jump, climb, and play games requiring these movement skills. Some adults consider this so-called "free play" meaningless. On the contrary, it is very meaningful to children as they explore various ways to move their bodies through space. In addition to this unorganized form of activity, there are various types of organized physical activity programs for children. In general, these can be classified into the two broad categories of (1) school programs, and (2) out-of-school programs.

School Programs. Most better-than-average elementary schools try to provide for well-balanced physical education programs for children. Just as young children need to learn the basic skills of reading, writing, and mathematics, they should also learn the basic physical skills. As mentioned in Chapter 3, these include: (1) locomotor skills, (2) auxiliary skills, and (3) skills of propulsion and retrieval.

For the young child, being able to move as effectively and efficiently as possible is directly related to the proficiency with which he or she will be able to perform the various fundamental physical skills. In turn, the success that children have in physical education activities requiring certain motor skills will be dependent upon their proficiency of performance of these skills. Thus, effective and efficient movement is prerequisite to the performance of basic motor skills needed for success in school physical education activities. These activities include active games, rhythmic activities and gymnastic activities.

Out-of-School Programs. Out-of-school programs are provided by various organizations such as boys' and girls' clubs and neighborhood recreation centers. These programs vary in quality depending upon the extent of suitable facilities and qualified personnel available to supervise and conduct them. Parents should investigate these programs thoroughly to make sure they are being conducted in the best interest of the children. This is mentioned because some highly competitive sports programs for children place more emphasis on adult pride than on the welfare of children. This should not be interpreted as an indictment against all out-of-school programs, because many of them are doing a commendable job.

Some families do not rely on any kind of organized out-of-school program, preferring instead to plan their own activities. They make a valid effort to provide activities on their own. This is commendable because it can make for fine family relationships as well as provide for wholesome physical activity for the entire family. There is much truth to the old adage: "The family that plays together stays together."

Up to this point this discussion has been concerned pretty much with school-age children. However, in recent years in keeping with the so-called "exercise craze," more and more emphasis has been placed on physical activity and exercise for "very tiny tots." In this regard it is interesting to note that the recommendation now seems to be that exercise in a planned manner should be a lifelong pursuit.

For the past several years the infant exercise concept has prompted widespread interest. One such program called *Gymboree* was started in 1976 by Joan Barnes, a former dance instructor from Burlingame, California. Growing at a very rapid rate, this program is divided into three sessions according to a child's age: (1) *BabyGym* — for infants three months to one year with parents helping their children with choreographed exercises such as bicycling legs or stretching arms; (2) *Gymboree* — for children from one year to 18 months with time devoted to "free exploration" and some structured time for songs, fingerplays and creative movements; and (3) *GymGrad* — for preschoolers two and one-half to four years using "Gymbercises," a combination of stretches, body awareness, and aerobics and following a different theme each week. Although lacking in solid scientific objective evidence to support its value, in general, parents have given much empirical support to this approach. Many parents report that after engaging in these activities with their children, they feel much more relaxed themselves. Thus, it is possible that this type of program provides for therapy for parents as well as the physical well-being of their children.

Rest and Sleep

To be effective in life pursuits, periodic recuperation is an essential ingredient in daily living patterns. Rest and sleep provide us with the means of revitalizing ourselves to meet the challenges of our responsibilities.

In order to keep fatigue at a minimum and in its proper proportion in the cycle of everyday activities, nature has provided us with ways that help combat and reduce it. (The reader should recall that the two types of fatigue — acute and chronic — were discussed in some detail in Chapter 5.)

Rest and sleep are essential to life as they afford the body the chance to regain its vitality and efficiency in a very positive way. Learning to utilize opportunities for rest and sleep may add years to our lives and zest to our years. Although rest and sleep are closely allied, they are not synonymous. For this reason it seems appropriate to consider them separately.

Rest. In general, most people think of rest as just "taking it easy." A chief purpose of rest is to reduce tension so that the body may be better able to recover from fatigue. There is no overt activity involved, but neither is there loss of consciousness as in sleep. In rest, there is no loss of awareness of the external environment as in sleep. Since the need for rest is usually in direct proportion to the type of activity in which we engage, it follows naturally that the more strenuous the activity, the more frequent the rest periods should be. A busy day at school may not be as noticeably active as a game of tennis, nevertheless, it is the wise person who will let the body dictate when a rest period is required. Five or ten minutes of sitting in a chair with eyes closed may make the difference in the course of an active day, assuming of course that this is possible. The real effectiveness of rest periods depends largely on the individual and his or her ability to let down and rest.

Sleep. Sleep is a phenomenon that has never been clearly defined or understood but it has aptly been described as the "great restorer." It is no wonder that authorities on the subject agree that sleep is essential to the vital functioning of the body and that natural sleep is the most satisfying form of recuperation from fatigue. It is during the hours of sleep that the body is given an opportunity to revitalize itself. All vital functions are slowed so that the building of new cells and the repair of tissues can take place without undue interruption. This does not mean that the body builds and regenerates tissue only during sleep, but it does mean that it is the time that nature has set aside to accomplish the task more easily. The body's metabolic rate is lowered and energy is restored.

Despite the acknowledged need for sleep, a question of paramount importance concerns the amount of sleep necessary for the body to accomplish its recuperative task. There is no clear-cut answer to this query. Sleep is an individual matter, based on degree rather than kind. The usual recommendation for adults is eight hours of sleep out of every 24, but the basis for this could well be one of fallacy rather than fact. There are many persons who can function effectively on much less sleep, while others require more. No matter how many hours of sleep you get during the course of a 24-hour period, the best test of adequacy will depend largely on how you feel. If you are normally alert, feel healthy, and are in good humor, you are probably getting a sufficient amount of sleep. The rest that sleep normally brings to the body depends to a large extent upon a person's freedom from excessive emotional tension and ability to relax. Unrelaxed sleep has little restorative value, but learning to relax is a skill that is not acquired in one night.

Is loss of sleep dangerous? This is a question that is pondered quite frequently. Again, the answer is not simple. To the normally healthy person with normal sleep habits, an occasional missing of the accustomed hours of sleep is not serious. On the other hand, repeated loss of sleep over a period of time can be dangerous. It is the loss of sleep night after night, rather than at one time, that apparently does the damage and results in the condition previously described as chronic fatigue. The general effects of loss of sleep are likely to result in poor general health, nervousness, irritability, inability to concentrate, lowered perseverance of effort, and serious fatigue. Studies have shown that a person can go for much longer periods of time without food than without sleep. In some instances successive loss of sleep for long periods have proven fatal. Under normal conditions, however, a night of lost sleep followed by a period of prolonged sleep will restore the individual to his normal self.

There are many conditions that tend to rob the body of restful slumber. Most certainly, mental anguish and worry play a very large part in holding sleep at bay. Some factors that influence the quality of sleep are hunger, cold, boredom, and excessive fatigue. Insomnia and chronic fatigue might well be brought to the attention of a physician so that the necessary steps can be taken to bring about restoration of normal sleep patterns. Certainly, drugs to induce sleep should be utilized only if prescribed by a physician.

Some recommendations about sleep might include: (1) relaxing physically and mentally before retiring, (2) reducing tension levels during the day, (3) managing your time, activities, and thoughts to prepare for a good night's sleep, and (4) the process should be the same each night, and should begin at the same hour, leading to repose at the same hour. That is, if one's bedtime is normally eleven o'clock preparation should perhaps begin at least by ten and probably not later than ten-thirty.

Sleeping Habits of Children

During the first year of a child's life it is a common practice to have two nap periods, one in the morning and one in the afternoon. The year-old child ordinarily, but gradually, gives up his morning nap and this tends to increase his afternoon nap time as well as his night sleep. With age the child will decrease his afternoon nap time, and as a consequence he will sleep longer at night. Although there is some difference of opinion on when a child should give up both the morning and afternoon nap, it is generally considered that preschoolers should have at least one nap a day, preferably in the afternoon.

As in the case of adults, school-age children differ in the number of hours of sleep required. The general recommendation is that on average out of every 24 hours they should get ten hours of sleep. A very important factor is that bedtime should be a happy time. Adults should not make such an issue of it that conflict results. Perhaps a good rule for a younger child is that he be "taken" to bed rather than "sent." The ceremony of reading or telling the child a pleasant story at bedtime is important and can help lessen the impact of sudden separation. It is important to remember that some of the sleep disorders of young children can be traced directly to stressful conditions under which separation at bedtime occurs.

It is important to remember that understanding the complex nature of sleep may be the province of scientists and other qualified experts, but an understanding of the value of sleep is the responsibility of everyone.

SCHOOL HEALTH

The field of school health is characterized by the somewhat unusual distinction of having a proposed list of standardized terms. Attempts at standardization of terminology in school health began many years ago through the efforts of the Health Education Section of what was then called the American Physical Education Association. Through the years many of the health education areas took on new meanings which made it necessary to redefine terms and clarify certain features in school health. The Committee on Terminology in School Health of the American Alliance for Health, Physical Education, Recreation, and Dance has carried out this function over the years.

The terminology and definitions of the various areas of school health used here are based as far as possible upon recommendations of this committee. However, it should be borne in mind that attempts to standardize terminology in such a rapidly changing and expanding area as school health precludes a static list of standardized terms. Consequently, terminology and descriptions or definitions of the various areas of school health will deviate from the committee's recommendations as seems necessary in terms of present theories and practices.

It is a generally accepted idea that the total *school health program* involves those school procedures that contribute to the understanding, maintenance, and improvement of the health of pupils and school personnel. In carrying out these functions the total school health program is composed of the three areas: *school health service, healthful school living,* and *school health education.* These three areas are interrelated and, to a large extent, interdependent; they are, however, obviously separate enough to warrant individual discussions.

School Health Service

The school health service program attempts to conserve, protect, and improve the health of the school population. This objective is achieved in part through such procedures as (1) appraising the health status of pupils and school personnel; (2) counseling with pupils, parents, and others involved in the appraisal findings; (3) helping to plan for the health care and education of exceptional children; (4) helping to prevent and control disease; and (5) providing for emergency care for sick and injured pupils.

The maximum function of school health service should provide all necessary health supervision to arrive at optimal health for all children. Naturally, such service depends upon the availability of specialized personnel such as physicians, nurses, psychologists, and others who can make worthwhile contributions to the health of children. The type and extent of service that is actually provided in a given school system also depends on such factors as available funds, size of school enrollment, and availability of properly trained personnel. Because of these factors, the range of school health services varies markedly from one school system to another.

The extreme importance of the health service aspect of the school health program is obvious when one considers the range of anomalous health conditions of the school population. For instance, some estimates indicate that, on the average, out of every one-hundred children of school age, one has heart disease, twenty have visual disorders, ten have some degree of hearing impairment, fifteen have nutritional disturbances, ten have some sort of growth problems, eighty-five have dental disease, and twenty have emotional disturbances. Added to these estimates are the facts that many children are only partially immunized, and countless others live under conditions of poor health practices that involve lack of sleep, fresh air, and sunshine.

Adequate school health services can do much to help eliminate these conditions. This is particularly true at the elementary school level because the younger the child is at the time a deviation from normal health is discovered, the greater the opportunity for proper care and possible recovery.

Role of the Classroom Teacher in School Health Service

Depending upon certain factors previously mentioned, the function of the classroom teacher in the school health service will vary from one school system to another. However, there are certain types of responsibilities that classroom teachers will likely be expected to assume in most elementary schools. Two of these major responsibilities follow.

Responsibilities concerned with health appraisal of children. Since teachers are in daily contact with children, coupled with their knowledge of growth and development, they are in an excellent position to note changes in appearance and behavior that are associated with a child's health status. When a teacher detects something that indicates a deviation from the normal health status, a referral can be made to the proper person in the health service (ordinarily the school nurse) who can follow up the referral.

Responsibilities concerned with emergency illness or injury. Ideally all school personnel should have an understanding of how to care for a child in case of sudden illness or injury. It is particularly important that the classroom teacher have the skills necessary to render first aid. One of the most important factors in this regard is a teacher's full understanding of the school's policy regarding emergency care. With such knowledge at hand, the teacher can administer first aid as set forth in the prescribed school policy.

Healthful School Living

This aspect of the school health program involves procedures that provide for the most satisfactory living conditions within the school plant. Healthful school living is concerned with (1) organizing the school day on a basis commensurate with the health and safety of pupils and (2) providing for physical aspects of the school plant—proper ventilation, heating, lighting, and the other aspects that are essential for preservation of an optimum health status.

As in the case of school health service, there is likely to be a wide range of standards of healthful school living among school systems. The standard of healthful living that a given school system provides will be governed largely by available funds and specialized personnel, particularly in the area of school maintenance.

Everyone in the school system should take some degree of responsibility for ensuring satisfactory healthful school living. The position of leadership in individual schools is, of course, that of the school principal. His or her awareness of the meaning of healthful school living and how to implement it depends, to a considerable extent, upon the success of this aspect of the school health program.

Although there is no question that the principal's leadership is of prime importance to the satisfactory conducting of this environmental aspect of the school health program, the importance of other personnel should not be underestimated. Thus, classroom teachers play a major role in seeing that they and their children participate in a satisfactory manner in the program. Moreover, the teacher is in an ideal position to keep the school administration sensitive to new problems and developments which require action that is beyond the teacher's scope or that of any individual class.

The children of the school, too, should be considered active participants in the maintenance of health school living, and, of course, the teacher can use this part of the school health program as a means of conveying basic principles of cleanliness and sanitation that are essential to group living.

The role of certain other personnel in the maintenance of healthful school living is so obvious as to require only brief mention in rounding out the total picture. Physicians, nurses, custodial staffs, food service personnel, and public health officers are all vitally concerned with healthful school living in the schools. Also, on occasion, problems may arise that require the attention of parent-teacher organizations as well as certain professional groups in the community.

SCHOOL HEALTH EDUCATION

It is the purpose of this aspect of the school health program to provide desirable and worthwhile learning experiences that will favorably influence knowledge, attitudes, and practices pertaining to individual and group health. The medium through which these experiences can best be provided is *health teaching*.

Without disputing the importance or even the indispensability of school health services and healthful living, it must be emphasized that health teaching which is designed to increase the individual's ability to live healthily and deal intelligently with his or her own health problems is basic to the whole concept of healthful living. Although some efforts are being made to procure special teachers it is quite clear that the major responsibility for health teaching in the elementary school rests with the classroom teacher. However, in many situations the teacher has numerous resources to draw upon in the way of materials and various health and safety personnel connected with either the school or the local public health organization. The teacher is responsible for utilizing these in such a way that they fit into the sequence of learning experiences.

Recognition of the importance of health teaching during the early years of life has gradually resulted in a national tendency to place greater emphasis upon health in the curriculum at all grade levels. More and more schools are making a definite effort to cover a series of health topics that are considered vital to the present and future health of the child. Many states have laws requiring that certain health topics be presented. These required topics were at first quite limited, commonly amounting to the effect of alcohol, tobacco, and narcotics upon the body. However, for several years now there has been a definite trend to go far beyond teaching only those health topics required by law.

In summary, there seems to be little question that the schools have a major responsibility in promoting optimum health for children, and thus, contributing to their total development.

BIBLIOGRAPHY

American Academy of Pediatrics, Physical fitness and the schools, *Pediatrics*, 80, 1987.

American College of Sports Medicine, Opinion statement of physical fitness in children and youth, *Medicine and Science in Sport and Exercise*, 4, 1988.

Armstrong, N. and Davies, B., The prevalence of coronary risk factors in children, *Acta Paediatrica Belgia*, 33, 1980.

Bar-Or, O., *Pediatric Sports Medicine*, M. Katz and E. R. Stehin (Eds.), New York, Springer-Verlag, 1983.

Blankenbaker, E. K., Development of perceptual-motor tasks, Yearbook (American Council on Industrial Arts Teacher Education), 1985.

Bossenmeyer, M., *Perceptual-Motor Development Guide*, Byron, CA, Front Row Experiences, 1988.

Brawley, L., Powers, and Phillips, K., Sex bias in evaluating motor activity: General or task-specific performance expectancy? *Journal of Sport Psychology*, 2, 1980.

Bridges, J. and DelCiampo, J., Children's perception of the competence of boys and girls, *Perceptual and Motor Skills*, 52, 1981.

Cartwright, C., Play can be the building blocks of learning, *Young Children*, July 1988.

Colonna, A. B. and Friedmann, M., Prediction of development, *The Psychoanalytic Study of the Child*, 39, 1984.

Cravens, H., Recent controversy in human development: A historical review, *Human Development*, November/December, 1987.

Duda, Marty, Prepubescent strength training gains support, *Physician and Sports Medicine*, 14, 1986.

Duncan, E. M., Whitney P., and Kunen, S., Integration of visual and verbal information in children's memories, *Child Development*, 53, 1982.

Dunn, J., Sibling influence on childhood development, *Journal of Child Psychology and Psychiatry and Allied Disciplines*, March 1988.

Frerichs, R. R., Srinivasan, S. R., Weber, L. S., and Berenson, G. S., Serum cholesterol and triglycerides levels, 3,446 children from a biracial community: The Bogalusa Heart Study, *Circulation*, 54, 1976.

Gabbard, C. P., The study of children's psychomotor behavior: A comprehensive program, *Journal of Physical Education, Recreation and Dance*, May/June 1985.

Garn, S. M. and LaVelle, M., Two decade follow-up of fatness in early childhood, *American Journal of Diseases in Children*, 139, 1985.

Gober, B. E. and Franks, B. D., Physical and fitness education of young children, *Journal of Physical Education, Recreation and Dance*, September 1988.

Herkowitz, J., Social-psychological correlates to motor development. In C. Corbin (Ed.), *A Textbook of Motor Development* (2nd ed.) Dubuque, Iowa, William C. Brown, 1980.

Horton, J. A. and Bailey, G. D., Visualization: Theory and application for teachers, *Reading Improvement,* 20, 1983.

Karnes, M. B., et al, Enhancing essential relationships: Developing a nurturing affective environment for young children, *Young Children,* November 1988.

Kee, D., Stovall, T., and Davis, B. R., Developmental changes in the effects of presentation mode on the storage and retrieval of noun pairs in children's recognition memory, *Child Development,* 52, 1981.

Klingsick, D., The whole child: Finding wholeness in community, *Lutheran Education,* March/April 1988.

Ladd, G. W., Enhancing our view of the child's social world: New territories, new maps, same directions? *Merrill-Palmer Quarterly,* July 1984.

Marks, I., The development of normal fear: A review, *Journal of Child Psychology and Psychiatry and Allied Disciplines,* September 1987.

Mead, C., Children's fears, *Forecast Home Economics,* November/December 1988.

Mozer, J. Child development as a base for decision-making, *Childhood Education,* May/June 1986.

Piechowski, M. M., The concept of developmental potential, *Roeper Review,* February 1986.

Pinnell, G. S. and Galloway, C. M., Human development, language and communication: Then and now, *Theory into Practice,* December 1987.

Robinson, S. L. and Nichols, M., In search of successful children, *Early Years,* January 1987.

Ross, G. J., Pate, R. R., Caspersen, C. J., Damberg, C. L., and Svilar, M., Home and community in children's exercise habits: The national children and youth fitness study II, *Journal of Physical Education, Recreation and Dance,* December 1987.

Ross, J. G., Pate, R. R., Lohman, T. G., and Christensen, G. M., Changes in the body composition of children, *Journal of Physical Education, Recreation and Dance,* December 1987.

Smuts, A. B. and Hagen, J. W., History and research in child development (symposium), *Monograph of the Society for Research in Child Development,* No 4–5, 1985.

Social cognition and the self system in early childhood (symposium) Ed. by J. A. Chafel, *Early Child Development and Care,* 1985.

Soderman, A. K., Dealing with difficult young children: Strategies for teachers and parents, *Young Children,* July 1985.

Strong, W. B., Atherosclerosis: Its pediatric roots, In N. M. Kaplan and E. Stamler Eds.), *Prevention of Coronary Heart Disease,* Philadelphia, W. B. Saunders, 1983.

The school's role in developing character (symposium), *Educational Leadership,* December 1985, January 1986.

The worlds of children (symposium), *Language Arts,* December 1986.

The young child at school (symposium), *Educational Leadership,* November 1986.

Tingey-Michaelis, C., Developing the whole child, *Early Years,* December 1984.

Tyson, R. L., The roots of psychopathology and our theories of development, *Journal of the American Academy of Child Psychiatry,* January 1986.

Wardle, F., Getting back to the basics of children's play, *Child Care Information Exchange,* September 1987.

Windholtz, G. and Lamal, P. A., Priority in the classical conditioning of children, *Teaching of Psychology,* December 1986.

INDEX